"As a teenager, it was reading [...] Jackie Pullinger that helped me i[...] be like. Reading Ann-Marie's [...] that. She has the same sense of [...] with huge trust in the God who has called her. Her ambition to eradicate FGM and resolute commitment through huge challenges is inspirational. Her faith is infectious. Read the book and it will likely rub off on you!"

Jonny Baker, CMS director of mission education

"Ann-Marie's life is a unique story of courage, perseverance, and professional excellence. Many of her extraordinary achievements at 28 Too Many have been accomplished as she has lived with, and fought through, the consequences of cancer. This book tells the story of a life full of energy and vision, and Ann-Marie's passion for ending FGM, which has had huge influence and impact in our generation, and will provide a rich legacy for the future."

Peter Grant, co-founder of Restored

"When faced with human suffering, the question 'What can I do?' is so overwhelming that many of us end up doing nothing. Ann-Marie's story shows what happens when someone learns from life's experiences, both the pleasurable and the painful, and takes them as opportunities to do something. We have known Ann-Marie for 20 years and watched the golden thread of compassion, 'to help the disadvantaged' weave its way with thoughtfulness, integrity and commitment through many different organizations and charities; she and her work leave an inspiring legacy for everyone who is tired of living a life of insignificance. As you read, let God speak to you about how your life can count too."

Revd John and Anne Coles

This book is dedicated to Fatima, whom I have known since 2005 and who is now likely to be twenty-six years old, hopefully with uncut children and grandchildren. Thank you for allowing me to fulfil my God-given calling, and to have the privilege of becoming a better person through birthing 28 Too Many. So, Fatima, if this book finds you, I hope your life is blessed and honoured. May we reunite, if God wills it.

This book is also dedicated to my eight godchildren: Anna, Fiona, Charlotte, Samantha, Zoe, Natalie, Michelle, and Jony. I hope this book will inspire you to be everything you can be, with a heart for those society can easily forget.

Also to the ten babies in Nigeria and Pakistan who gave me the privilege of becoming a midwife. Thank you for allowing me to fulfil my maternal instinct by bringing you into the world.

Text copyright © 2021 Ann-Marie Wilson
This edition copyright © 2021 Lion Hudson IP Limited

The right of Ann-Marie Wilson to be identified as the author of this work has been asserted by her in accordance with the Copyright, Designs and Patents Act 1988.

Published by Lion Hudson Limited

Wilkinson House, Jordan Hill Business Park
Banbury Road, Oxford OX2 8DR, England
www.lionhudson.com

ISBN 978 1 80030 007 1
e-ISBN 978 1 80030 025 5
First edition 2021

Acknowledgments
Scripture quotation taken from The Holy Bible, New International Version®, NIV®
Copyright © 1973, 1978, 1984, 2011 by Biblica, Inc.® Used by permission. All rights reserved worldwide.
A catalogue record for this book is available from the British Library

Printed and bound in the UK, May 2021, LH26

Overcoming

MY FIGHT AGAINST FGM

DR ANN-MARIE WILSON

To margaret
May you always overcome all
with God's help

Ann-Marie
x.

M
MONARCH

Acknowledgments

It seems incredible to me how a book that has been sitting in my head for twenty years has found its way onto the page and is now available for you to learn a little more about my journey.

I would like to take a moment to say thank you to everyone who truly supported this book.

Firstly, the teachers and educators throughout my life who have instilled in me a love of communication and the written word. Thanks to my high-school friend, Christine, who took me to her writing group in Hawaii fifteen years ago and, as an author, encouraged me to never give up. And to the leaders of the Macmillan cancer writing group at University College London Hospital – Wendy, Genevieve, and Vikky – as well as the other members, for helping me hone my skills over the last five years.

Thank you to Andrea, Selina, and Ebony, my PAs, and to Jo, Grace, Mel, and Yvonne, who helped edit the book. Also to Emma, who contributed to the cover design and sifted through countless photos for the image plate. Thanks to all my loving friends and family who have supported me as I have written this book: in particular, David and the board of 28 Too Many; Tanas and Philip, my long-suffering managers at Church Mission Society; the leaders and congregations of my home and link churches across the UK; and last, but by no means least, the team at Lion Hudson – particularly Suzanne, Josh, and Joy – for their honesty, courtesy, and professionalism in achieving a 2021 publishing date, despite the challenges of 2020.

CONTENTS

INTRODUCTION

She stood in a doorway with her newborn in her arms, wearing her best dress and a pair of simple sandals, a small bag by her side. I smiled and she gave me a wan smile in return. Her baby was only a few weeks old, yet she had been asked to travel by truck to live with a distant auntie (her late mother's cousin) in the far south of Sudan.

Just a few weeks beforehand, we had found "Fatima", a ten-year-old girl, alone in the scrubland of West Darfur. We had been travelling out from our medical camp during a visit to a nearby community project. Fatima was at least seven months pregnant, and we learned she had conceived at the age of ten, following a rape carried out by the Janjaweed militia. She had been left for dead, and was the only person to survive the armed raid that had left her family, village, and community dead. Rape was commonly used in the West Darfur conflict as a way of subjugating the people, and for ethnic cleansing reasons.

Fatima was alone. She had experienced infibulation, a Type III female genital mutilation (FGM), at five years old, having been sewn up to preserve her purity for marriage.[1] We gave her a safe delivery and arranged for her to be sent to her nearest relative, whom she had never met.

I looked at her, worried about her future. Fatima had survived female genital mutilation, a form of child abuse, at the age of five. By the age of ten she had been a victim of conflict rape. She faced obstructed labour, trauma, and complications

---

1   I will explain more about female genital mutilation, infibulation, and
      deinfibulation in Chapter Three.

7

in childbirth, and problems with sexual intimacy for the rest of her life. She may also have ended up with a fistula (a tear, which leads to incontinence) in future pregnancies. It seemed unlikely that Fatima would make a good union, as she was unchaste. She was likely to become a fourth wife and servant to an older wife in her extended family, or to be sold on to another, probably older, man.

What could I do? As a white, London-based human resources consultant, I was neither doctor nor nurse. I spoke only a smattering of Arabic and Swahili, and I wasn't sure how I could help stop this happening to other girls like Fatima. I called out to God and asked, "Who will help girls like this?" To my amazement, I heard an audible voice say, "You will."

I wasn't sure what to make of this, but I extended my Sudanese visa and headed back to Kenya for a short trip to our aid work head office. As it turned out, I broke my foot that weekend and flew back to the UK as planned. While I was recovering, planning to return, I learned that Darfur's troubles had escalated, and that all non-essential staff were being sent out from the project. As I nursed my broken foot, I had more time to think about Fatima – in fact, I couldn't get her out of my mind. It was as if a shard of glass had pierced my heart and could not be dislodged.

Over the last twenty years of focusing on FGM, forced marriage, reproductive health, and gender-based violence, I have come to understand the roots of FGM, including its links to patriarchy and misogyny. I have become clearer on what works and what doesn't in different development contexts.

Despite not initially wanting to run my own charity, 28 Too Many, it became clear that this was a necessary step to raise the funds needed to complete the work. My life experience as an entrepreneur, psychologist, coach, and board member enabled me to put into action many of the skills required to launch the charity, which happened in 2012 – two years after the full-time project started. I used the first two years as a time of training, and was accountable under the umbrella of Church Mission Society (CMS) as a pioneer in its Africa team.

I was lucky enough to be awarded a Tearfund Inspired Individual scholarship from 2011–15. The four years of mentoring, training, and support, alongside other pioneer charity leaders in the making, helped me avoid the burnout that would likely otherwise have followed the long hours and overseas travel.

As 28 Too Many grew, the board meeting of four trustees around my kitchen table in 2012 made way for a board of ten at pro bono London offices. The board grew and was shaped, moulded, and reshaped into the professional board we have today. During this season, I spent up to four months a year in Africa, clocking up fourteen African country visas on my passport, and a TripAdvisor rating of having visited more than 60% of the planet.

Just as every collection of stories contains great joy and amazing examples of hope, there are also accounts of hardship and setbacks. Colleagues have come and gone; some non-governmental organizations (NGOs) have chosen not to collaborate; reputation challenges have been contested; and risky opportunities have been offered – some of which did not pay off. Friendships in this sector have waxed and waned, but all the while our work has grown in reputation and become increasingly useful to high-profile users of our reports.

We became known for our two-pronged approach to ending FGM: first, to provide research that would inform change agents, country leaders, the UN, European and UK governments, faith leaders, and influencers (such as educationalists, health workers, the police, and social workers); second, to provide resources and training presentations for local activists to use to help end FGM in their communities, and then to help them advocate for countrywide change.

We produced reports on each of the twenty-eight countries in Africa that practise FGM, which have since been updated with an expanded scope to include the existing law in each country. We have also produced thematic reports on FGM and medicalization, social norms, and thirty reports on the law, with other specialist reports to follow. Our website was revamped twice in six years, and has finally become the research portal of my dreams, translated into several languages. This has enabled many more of our target beneficiary groups – vulnerable girls at risk of FGM, professionals, policymakers, NGOs in Africa, and change agents – to access pertinent information and make sound decisions.

I look back to 2005, when I first felt called to stand up for girls and women like Fatima. My heart's work has now reached the age of a teenager! I feel privileged to have listened to more than 3,000 stories of girls and women who have survived FGM, many of whom have gone on to be thriving survivors, activists, and campaigners with a desire to stop it happening to the next generation. I have seen the movement come of age and birth initiatives, such as roles for men and boys in ending FGM. Most of the survivors were not vocal about their own FGM when I started in 2005, yet their daughters have remained uncut.

All was going well until 2015, when I was suddenly and completely unexpectedly diagnosed with cancer. Following my diagnosis, the charity wobbled. Most of our team had joined as volunteers, and for various reasons almost all of them left fairly soon after I was diagnosed. It may have all been a coincidence, but it felt fairly dire, as it became impossible for me to take any time off work during my treatment because I felt the charity would collapse if I did. Within seven months of my diagnosis we had regrouped the board. We had an acting chair and chair-in-waiting, and a new deputy who helped recruit or cover key roles. The ship restabilized, and it has gone from strength to strength.

Having cancer has given me a better perspective on the trauma and on the physical and mental impact of FGM, as I too cope with chronic issues. I have also campaigned for various disability rights, such as creating the "Please give me a seat" badge for Transport for London. I have joined various disability campaigns for palliative care rights, better clinical trials, and accessible transport. I have enjoyed being a research subject for PhD students, authors, and those in media. I have widened my fundraising skills, from the £1 million I helped raise for Medair and the annual £150,000 for 28 Too Many's needs to dressing up for a Santa Run – completed with sticks and a wheelchair. I also reframed the Brighton Marathon that I could not complete in March 2015 by designing my own, with a twenty-eight-mile route in the shape of Africa. I was pushed in a wheelchair by twenty-eight teams, each representing an FGM-researched country. The forty people involved raised more than £20,000!

The charity will always be my baby, yet it is now one of ten legacy projects I plan to complete by 2022. We are looking at future options for the charity, which I will share later in this book.

I conclude with tips on how to get involved with 28 Too Many yourself. Buying this book has already taken you one step in the right direction, with all my profits from the book going toward our work to end FGM and violence against women.

ONE:
YOUTHFUL AMBITION

I am often asked, "How do I find my calling?" In my own life, I have always found it is easier to look back reflectively and see what patterns can be discerned.

I come from a line of entrepreneurial men and women. My paternal grandmother ran a boot and shoe shop in Manchester in 1900, so my father was privileged to have boots without holes, as opposed to ones that were lined with newspapers to keep the feet as dry as possible. My maternal grandfather was a carpenter who made joinery tools and built his own house in 1920s Birmingham. This meant my mother sorted screws, nails, and washers in glass jars from a young age, and ran the bookkeeping from the age of twelve. My uncle also joined the business, so most of my household furniture was hand-carved by family members.

My father planned to start a business in post-war Palestine with an Arab partner and his Jewish fiancée, selling war munitions abandoned in the desert, but this fell through after the Suez Crisis. My mother worked for the civil service, retrained as a cordon bleu cookery trainer and taught domestic science to adults at a technical college in High Wycombe after she married my father, and then worked as a bookkeeper from the time I started school, dedicating the last twenty-five years of her life to the profession – the last six on a self-employed basis.

Seeing different businesses during my early years fuelled my interest in life beyond the village I had grown up in. As a child of five in 1967, I announced to my family that I wanted to be a surgeon, perhaps because I had enjoyed my plastic doctor and nurse kit a little too much! I joined the Red Cross a year later and loved it – the skills exams, the MENCAP holiday clubs, volunteering at a retired nurses' home, and more – and I continued with this activity until I left for university. I was chosen to represent the Buckinghamshire branch of the Red Cross on a Russian exchange at the age of sixteen, which was a life-changing experience, and my Duke of Edinburgh's Gold Award was presented by the duke for my contribution to the Red Cross and pseudo medical-related service.

A bright all-rounder, I particularly enjoyed the sciences as a youngster. After spending six years at a convent school, I passed the eleven-plus, which enabled me to attend a girls' grammar school. When it came to choosing options at the age of fourteen, my last choice was to take either needlework and dress-making, or cookery. Having taught domestic science, my mother encouraged me to take needlework. Her philosophy was that anyone could follow a recipe, but that needlework was a skill that needed to be taught. As a result, I can make my own clothes (yet choose not to) and was taught cookery by my cordon bleu cookery trainer mother (although I have very few dinner parties these days). Both offered vital survival skills overseas in later life when provisions were scarce!

Becoming a surgeon seemed increasingly unlikely by the time I turned fourteen. I hadn't transitioned well from the convent's traditional science teaching to the grammar school's Nuffield curriculum. How was I supposed to work out the colour of one planet from the colour of another? I still wonder about that!

I revised my career options, deciding to become an occupational therapist instead, and life seemed to be taking me down the required path. Then a few things happened that changed my overall destiny. The sister of a very close friend took her own life, which made me question the value of study and hampered my motivation. I didn't really know how to study or see why I should. I also started a relationship with the brother of this friend. I underperformed in my O levels (GCSEs), but had attended various careers taster sessions: one for a physiotherapy rehabilitation unit run by a friend's father; one with Caledonian Airways to become a stewardess; and one at a high street bank's model bank training site in Teddington. Weirdly, I loved being locked into the bank and running it for a day. I made a mental shift, recognizing that I could help people via various non-medical routes.

The world of work

My O level results were good enough for me to do A levels in Biology, French, and English, yet I had set my heart on Economics and needed Bs in Maths and English instead of an A and C, respectively. The school was not as convinced as I was that they averaged out!

I talked to a friend's father, who happened to be a director at the bank. I was quite nervous going to see him in the drawing room rather than chilling out with his daughter in the kitchen. At the end of the meeting, he said that it was fine to leave school if I wanted to work in business, as I could take exams in banking while I worked. I ordered the application forms, went to a local branch, and was offered a job in the same town as my secondary school. I felt I had outgrown my local neighbourhood and was ready to spread my wings, so I rejected the job and applied for one at a north-west London branch. This was also successful. I learned that the local day-release course was enrolling at High Wycombe College, so I signed up before starting work in Edgware Road.

I learned a lot at the bank. Out of the three boys and three girls, only the boys and I were enrolled at the college. The HR manager seemed annoyed that I had signed up. Sometime later I was tested on my encoding skills, and I chose to do all the easy items in the pile first to reduce the task by 50%. Unfortunately, the test only seemed to count the most difficult ones!

As a slow typist – not having learned to type at school – I was transferred to the regional head office. I suddenly fitted in again and was valued. The significance of what I was doing was explained to me, and I began to understand the bigger picture.

By the age of seventeen I had experienced the different expectations the bank had of men and women. My enlightened college statistics tutor counselled me and said that I had already hit a glass ceiling and would face many more. Girls were expected to work in the machine room and marry bankers, who took the exams. Boys only had to do a week of encoding before being appointed as cashiers, while girls remained data input clerks for years, or until they married bankers.

I studied hard and loved my work and study, as I could see the relevance of both. I applied to university to take business studies and was accepted under the proviso that I achieved a distinction in my business BTEC (which was equivalent to three A levels). It was not easy to gain a university place without A levels, yet I received a number of offers. I chose Manchester, as that was where my father's family was from, and I hoped I might be able to reconnect with some relatives we hadn't seen for a long time owing to the geographical distance.

Choosing a business degree gave me an all-round understanding of work. I found it difficult to select from the list of first-year options, so I chose to learn German from scratch and manufacturing technology. This led to a five-month placement in Germany with two other students from my course.

We were placed in a German steel factory making dye moulds. I loved it, and we lived in an apartment in the top penthouse suite of a hotel. The Falklands War broke out while we were there in April 1982. We heard the announcement on British Forces radio, and it sounded as if the UK had been invaded.

We were befriended by a missionary couple and their family, who hosted us for church and a tea of American waffles on a weekly basis. My time in Germany certainly wasn't just tea and waffles, however, as I recall the factory's chief executive showing an unhealthy interest in me. He would request my presence in his office each week, and being young and naive I felt flattered to be singled out. I chose not to tell anyone, as my tutor had told me how important this placement was for the university. I dealt with favouritism, sexism, grooming, and cross-cultural and religious issues during my time in Germany, as well as noticing the differences between the way factory and office workers were treated. The experience took years to mentally process and recover from.

In my third year I was pleased to be offered a one-year placement with Marks & Spencer (M&S). I delivered electronic point of sale (EPOS) training to cashier staff, looked after recruitment and staffing, and learned basic retail skills in men's underwear with my trusted tape measure! I was in charge of Christmas gifts, January returns, and inspecting food hygiene in the staff restaurant. I also produced a purple outfit that turned out to be top of the winter range. At an M&S pie factory, I learned about the relationships suppliers have with their buyers. It was my experiences at this pie factory – where pigs came in and pies left – that led to lifelong vegetarianism.

The skills I gained at M&S were invaluable – learning to get along with many different people from diverse backgrounds, and to work in a culture where all stores operated as copies of each other. For example, all pay rises were announced at 8 a.m. on a set date across all stores.

I returned to the bank during my fourth-year summer holidays (having also worked there during my second-year summer holidays), and was a well-paid student, meaning I graduated without any debt and with enough money to buy a brand new car.

My father was dying by the end of my degree. I needed to be closer to home, so I chose an HR trainee role in the south-east region at British Gas, passing the two-day assessment at a centre in Stratford. We were observed continuously, and even my gesture of offering my room to a man whose room was not ready but who needed to change may have raised eyebrows, as I had been put in the four-poster honeymoon suite! Dinner involved a debate on the miners' strike – a topic dear to me, given that I had spent so much time in Manchester. Assessors and applicants were alternated around fancy dinner tables, and I tried to help a guy who had no idea which cutlery to use. In hindsight, I'm sure all of this was also noted.

I chose to join British Gas because it was a mixed, blue-collar industry, although it became a private limited company during the summer between receiving my offer and joining. I drove my new car from my parents' home to my new job in Croydon. I got lost in Brixton and had to ask for directions. It wasn't much like the area I had grown up in, but wasn't dissimilar to parts of Manchester I was familiar with.

My mother and I nursed my father between May and November 1985, when he sadly died. I moved in with my boyfriend immediately after his death, not realizing at the time that I saw him as a sort of replacement father figure. We were engaged in 1987 and married in 1988.

While at British Gas, I signed up for personnel management exams and stayed on after graduation to study for a diploma in marketing – and to do a parachute jump! I had taken joint honours in marketing and HR, hoping to go into HR, although I would have been happy with either career branch. I ended up working in training – focusing on dreams and values, the two core areas I had studied. By this time I already had four years' work experience, which was by far the most useful part of my CV.

The head of HR at British Gas was a visionary and suggested that, as I would be spending the rest of my career in HR, it would be best to use the first year to familiarize myself with the business. So I divided the year between finance, marketing, transmission, and distribution, spending three months in each sphere. Tasks included going out in an unmarked van to cut off the gas supply in the street for those who could not pay their bills; emptying slot meters; sending out bills; appearing on the Ideal Home Show exhibition stand; baking cakes at gas showrooms; digging a hole in the road; working on the pipeline inspection gadget (PIG) line under the sea; and flying offshore from Morecambe Bay. I learned how to survive the nude calendars and Page 3 posters, the lack of female toilets on site, the big cooked breakfasts yet no lunch, and, most importantly, how to relate to a wide variety of people.

These were the people I worked with for the next four years as a personnel recruitment officer, in training and equal opportunities, and at head office. I negotiated with the trade union and sat in on disciplinary cases where engineers had stolen a rod of copper pipe to do their own plumbing. I recruited apprentices – the same type of lads I had attended apprentice workshop training and college with in Germany. I quickly moved from personnel (all about rules) to training (all about possibilities).

My manager said, "You'll never make it here unless you prove you can break the unions." I believed there were other ways. I dreamed of, and was appointed to, my mentor's job in training, and went from there to equal opportunities, and finally to head office. I had five jobs in five years, and only left because I was told I was too young at twenty-eight to become a senior manager. If I had been told I was too inexperienced I might still be there, but to me age was irrelevant. I applied for various senior internal roles, including complaints handler for the chairman. They couldn't believe I had used no rough paper for a draft complaint letter, as I had written the final form straight from my head!

During my year at M&S, and my five years at British Gas, I learned what I liked and disliked from an employer in terms of rules, authority, power, spans of control, leadership, management, equality, and ethics. I also experienced the way an employer handled personal issues after my dad died.

Shortly after leaving British Gas, I saw a vacancy for a marketing manager in graduate recruitment at KPMG. Moving to a City accountancy partnership was another culture change, where only partnership experience was valid. I was to recruit the brightest and best – at any cost, with more than twenty staff, my own office, and a bottomless budget. The first thing I did was set a budget to see what return I was getting on our investment in the various PR projects – cricket covers at Durham University, lacrosse team bags at Exeter, and the like. It was perfect for me.

For three years I gained a higher proportion of the best, and on results day one summer I was featured in *The Sunday*

Times. As it was August, the partner, director, and senior manager of the HR department were all away on holiday. I agreed to an interview, and they asked if a photographer could come and take a photo. After looking at my basement office in Puddle Dock, they asked about other offices, so I naively took them up to the partners' top floor offices. As each partner chose his own office, furniture, and PA, each looked different.

We wandered the corridors of power and the photographer picked an old-school style office. He made me go behind the desk and lean forward as he shot me from the floor upwards. Well, the finished photo was half a broadsheet – and I looked very powerful. I was called in on the Monday and told not to do that again, though the partner and others I knew from synagogue (and my mum!) were secretly impressed.

The greatest challenge was the recession, which in the first year meant I had to be involved in bringing final-year students back to the office to be made redundant. The second year meant the post of my colleague who was on maternity leave was made redundant, and I was given a £5,000 increase to cover her role. In the third year I had to make plans for my team members to be made redundant. I hated escorting them around to clear their desks and leave.

Sadly, my mum died not long after this, and I took two months off to process my grief. In my absence, I was told that my own role was in jeopardy.

New directions

On my first day back at work, I realized my desk had moved! I was relocated to a new building without a role, so I decided to use the opportunity to start my own business. I attended courses on vision and creativity, read books, received coaching, and designed letterheads and business cards. After a six-month secondment to the Mental Health Foundation, I was approached by a colleague at another firm to take on an HR role in Prague for five months, followed by another in Bratislava. My role was to train a Russian-speaking engineer to become an English-speaking personnel manager. She sat with me daily as I wrote European policies and an HR handbook. Three evenings a week she was tutored in English by an American. We ended up becoming a close trio, as I dated the tutor on his evenings off and spent weekends with my trainee's family – learning about the hard life of the Czech people under the previous regime. I saw alcoholism and obesity as men drank litre glasses of beer for breakfast. It was no wonder their wives needed friends to go to the theatre or out walking with.

I learned about professional practices and set up my business to offer HR services to firms, housing providers, charities, and national and local government agencies. I easily found work with a law firm and managed all the graduate recruitment of another accountancy firm. I had benefitted from working for four blue chip companies before setting up my own firm, and the recession meant businesses were looking to outsource various HR functions. I liked working for myself rather than the City, as I set my own values. I only accepted the projects I chose, and didn't have to do any nasty HR! I was following in the entrepreneurial footsteps of my parents and two of my grandparents, and once back from Bratislava I focused on developing the business. I joined Business Link, under the Chamber of Commerce, and wrote a monthly column on either HR or marketing.

During my early thirties, my ten-year marriage, which had begun just before graduation, came to an end. My mum had been diagnosed with cancer during our honeymoon, so, having helped her through her grief, redundancy, shingles, and poor mental health after my father's death, I then supported her through chemotherapy, mastectomy, and radiotherapy. I had also supported my Jewish husband through his PhD, and we had moved to north London to be nearer his parents and his new job.

He was difficult to live with, yet I chose to convert to Judaism so we could have a faith in common. Despite being only a convert, I had a full role in the Jewish community, where I became a member of the Synagogue Council and the Reform Board Synagogues in the UK. With a challenging job, a demanding husband, an engaging Jewish life, the recent loss of my father, and an unwell mother to look after, there had been very little time for myself. It was hardly surprising that I needed time to recover after my mother died, and that the strain was more than the marriage could sustain.

My business thrived, as I had corporate experience and was willing to offer it to the not-for-profit sector at a low cost. I set it up as a break-even business, with some clients paying a lot, some a little, and some nothing at all. I supplemented my fledgling business by teaching business studies at Barnet College. Ironically, I was also drafted in to teach A level economics, as the tutor's daughter had been diagnosed with leukaemia. I was soon teaching on a BA course in marketing communications at the University of Hertfordshire, and on HR at the University of Westminster. These roles could be fitted around my recovery from grief and sorting out my life as I faced separation and then divorce.

I wasn't in a position to fight a legal battle, so my husband received a very generous settlement of nearly half my inheritance, but at least it gave me a clean break. I felt bad that my parents' retirement funds had been used to pay off the negative equity of my husband's new wife, yet I couldn't face the legal battle required to contest the decision in court. I knew he would have preferred the lawyers to take all the money than to offer me a better settlement.

I chose to volunteer on various executive boards at this time. I joined Metropolitan Housing Trust as an experienced HR trustee and stayed for around eight years, becoming chair of the north-west region, addressing staff away days, chairing complaints, making awards, negotiating pay, and sitting on disciplinary panels. I also joined InterHealth Worldwide, People in Aid, and, Medair, all for three to five years. These roles gave me excellent board experience – which turned out to be a great benefit for 28 Too Many – and complemented the experience I had gained as a consultant in addressing boards over messy HR assignments.

I had undertaken a counselling skills certificate and diploma during the 1990s, and later took a diploma in business coaching. These gave me an introduction to neurolinguistic programming (NLP) – a psychological approach to communication and development, using language to reprogramme the brain – which I found helpful in assisting clients and employees to achieve their chosen outcome. I was pleased that all the complaints received on my watch at Metropolitan Housing Trust ended satisfactorily. Having insisted on seeing each complainant at their home before the hearing, I realized people needed to be listened to more than they needed compensation.

After six years of running my own consultancy, I had six staff members and felt I had more or less replicated the situation at KPMG, only I was busy doing lots of activities I liked less, such as running the business. I met a woman via my NLP network who was keen to leave corporate banking and run her own business. Her husband was an ex-bank manager, which meant that he could run our finances and office while she and I delivered HR recruitment or training solutions, offering a wider range of services. I could also train in NLP at master and trainer level, and we could offer qualification-level courses to delegates. The main appeal of this new partnership was that it gave me time to dedicate to my volunteer roles, so we joined forces in September 1999.

Volunteering

I had planned a sabbatical in Indo-China and the Pacific Rim for three months, working with girls in the sex industry in Thailand and with women entrepreneurs in Vietnam; teaching English to Buddhist priests in Laos; and visiting children in Cambodian orphanages. The week before I left, I decided to become a committed Christian, having just completed an Alpha Course at Holy Trinity Brompton church under Revd Nicky Gumbel.

I had always had a faith, possibly inspired by the nuns at the convent. Despite being sexually abused by a priest at school,

I maintained my faith in an all-powerful Father God. By the age of seven or eight I was inquisitive, and asked my parents if I could go to a Church of England Sunday school. From the age of twelve I attended with a friend and her mum, and we were confirmed together. I loved projects, so it came as no surprise that I won the confirmation journal prize! I was given a 1970s *Good News Bible* for my efforts, which I covered in peace, love, and fish-shaped stickers! Sadly, I couldn't get my head around Jesus and the Holy Spirit. I was particularly wary of the Holy Spirit, having been put off by talk of the Holy Ghost and purgatory from our keen but inexperienced religious education assistant at the convent.

I attended church throughout my teens, subsequently joining a university student church in Platt Fields, Manchester, where I enjoyed the jacket potatoes and fellowship after the Sunday evening service. Despite having a steady Jewish boyfriend and a Muslim friend from Mensa, I kept my own faith and returned to church with my mum at Christmas and Easter. After I married and converted to Judaism, I remember telling Mum in tears that I couldn't take Communion any more. My mum's fervour had waned, but I encouraged her to embrace a full, born-again faith, which enabled her to blossom. Meanwhile, I was thriving in the Jewish community and with my husband's family. My mum was amazingly accommodating, making me an embroidered challah (bread) cover, and buying me a cookery book for my conversion Jewish wedding.

After my marriage ended, I explored Islam, New Ageism, an Indian sect (Sri Chinmoy) via meditation classes, and Buddhism. I finally decided, on the advice of the Dalai Lama, to look at my own faith, and joined the Alpha course. About 1,000 people attended on a Monday and another 1,000 on a Wednesday, all from just one church, Holy Trinity Brompton (HTB) in London.

My Alpha leader had been born with incompletely formed hands, with two fingers on each shoulder, yet he perfectly balanced a plate in one hand and a cup of coffee in the other, then asked me to hold one so we could shake hands. He was a great course leader, and as I had some follow-up questions after session four, and his journey home took him past my house, he offered me a lift.

On the way, he told me a great miraculous story about his son, who had been born profoundly deaf. He remembers praying to God, saying that he was sad because he wasn't able to sign well. He heard God say, "*Speak* to your son!" When he replied with, "Sorry God, but you remember he can't hear?!" God repeated the phrase again. And when he did speak to his son, who was four by this point, the little boy said, "Stop shouting, Daddy!" The boy's records state "miraculous cure", and there are X-rays showing that there is no mechanism in his head to enable hearing. Hearing about this miracle helped my baby Christian faith grow to a point of commitment.

After that I was ready to see what God wanted me to do with my life. I had taken an initial capital down payment from my business partner, which would cover the payroll for this three-month period if the business failed. It didn't fail, however; it thrived for three years.

I took three months off each year, which enabled me to do voluntary aid work. I also committed to a PsyD/PhD in psychology, starting in 2001 (after a busy 2000 growing our business). By 2003, I was committed to three months of aid work and a further three months of studying for my doctorate. My partner was committed to maximizing our business prior to her retirement, so we went our separate ways, which meant I was free to work overseas.

My biggest honour during this period occurred while I was on a trip to Nairobi, having been asked by my boss to go to a meeting about setting up civil service policies for the new state of South Sudan. I bought a navy dress and shoes from the second-hand clothes market – both originally from Marks & Spencer – and headed to a posh hotel. We were divided into four groups, with a man chairing each. Interestingly, a woman was expected to scribe each group and I was selected as group scribe, which involved taking notes and feeding back on our discussions.

The two presidents-elect of Sudan and South Sudan, Omar al-Bashir and John Garang (who sadly died in a plane crash) were there. Omar al-Bashir commented, "I see this as a good omen for the new state of South Sudan that women will lead." As almost the only white woman at the conference, I had to pinch myself to believe I was really there at all, helping to form policy at country level. It was a bit like being invited to 10 Downing Street.

I also worked in North Sudan, where I caught a nasty dose of giardiasis, which followed me from there to Uganda and then on to Kenya. An upturned sheep had been cooked on a grill in the open air in upstate Khartoum, and I ate some with a watery sauce. I was suddenly aware of the need to be sick, but wasn't able to make it to the latrines. I vomited into our office waste bin – how humiliating! I couldn't eat any bread or water, and was sick again on a trip to the villages, squatting behind our Land Rover. We had no laboratory tests, but I was eventually given antibiotics and felt better for a short while. My illness came back without warning in Nairobi in the form of diarrhoea while walking up a shopping mall escalator. The next day, the doctor confirmed giardiasis. I asked her what had caused it and she said, "You have consumed human excrement." Joy!

I also had salmonella at one point. I contemplated my ills the whole night in the latrine. Devotions that evening had been on the book of Lamentations, and I could relate to it all too well.

Illness in the field is quite common, and I usually had to take de-worming tablets in Nairobi. I had managed to avoid the nasty bugs from stagnant water that burrowed into toes, despite having to wade up to my waist through a river in South Sudan. I also avoided malaria. Unfortunately, I contracted brucellosis – a farmer's disease – in Sudan, also from inhaling airborne excrement. Still, this wasn't a bad health record from nearly twenty years of aid work.

I carried on as a self-employed aid worker after returning from Sudan in 2005 until I joined a mission agency in 2010. During this interim period I worked in Mozambique, South Africa, Myanmar, Thailand, China, the USA, Sweden, Pakistan, Nigeria, and Belarus.

Apart from consolidating my calling, these experiences helped me use my secular and professional skills in faith and cross-cultural contexts. The time spent exploring a general calling (1999–2005) and refining a specific calling and building a vision (2005–10) enabled me to reflect on mistakes and obstacles to success; redeeming opportunities and relationships, and turning them into learning. I built confidence and psychological resilience, and became more grounded in my faith.

TWO:
EARLY DAYS IN
AID WORK

I was offered an HR consultant role at hmanitarian aid organization Medair's head office in Lausanne, Switzerland, and, from there, a training assignment in Kenya for the South Sudan team that December. I felt flattered, but was concerned that I had no aid experience. The CEO suggested Madagascar for a summer visit "as the weather is very nice then". The much more pragmatic Dutch operations director said, "She's far too useful for that – we'll drop her into Kosovo." So my Easter vacation at head office doing an HR audit turned into a summer vacation in Kosovo. Here began my aid sector season of life, which spanned the next twenty years.

I stayed at the house of the NGO's founders, as we were booked on an early military flight from Basel the next day. The plane was stripped of almost all its seats and was full of kit. We were the only two civilians on board – the rest were soldiers from the Swiss Army, all sleeping at the end of their tour.

On arrival, I handed over an envelope of Deutschemarks to the military officer in the arrivals area, which looked like a khaki bouncy castle. We had landed in the Italian quarter. The soldiers there were stylish, sunning themselves behind their expensive sunglasses as they leaned nonchalantly against their impressive-looking vehicles. We were collected by the logistician and driven through streets with sandbags on either side of the temporary traffic lights and armed guards in full combat gear holding Kalashnikovs. It reminded me of visits I had made to Belfast during the late 1980s.

After a brief introduction to the team and time for a quick unpack, we were told we were going to a United Nations reception and were whisked off in our smartest clothes. Classical music was playing on a gramophone and we were offered sherry and canapés. I headed to bed to sleep in the hot room I was sharing with the female founder, as we had another early start the next day and I was finding it hard to process all my cross-cultural experiences.

My time in Kosovo was full of challenge and learning. It was a completely new experience on many levels, and the memories are just as fresh now, with many bringing a smile to my face. I shadowed the logistics manager and saw the projects the NGO was delivering in Pristina. After watching the Romanian children's crisis develop during the later 1990s, I had promised God I would be ready to go to the next crisis, which just happened to be Kosovo. War had broken out there several years earlier, in March 1999, and instead of knitting blankets or driving a truck to Romania – the only useful skills I could see to offer there – I found myself using my coaching, counselling, and debriefing skills in Kosovo with a team of four managers who were seriously burned out from four years of life in a war zone.

I clearly remember the day we met an elderly Albanian man whose house had lost its roof in the bombings. We were there to provide a temporary tarpaulin roof followed by a more permanent solution, which would enable him to work to pay for a proper new roof. His wife had died during the war and his son had fled to Germany. He refused the new roof, saying, "There is only my daughter and me here – we don't need it." We could not force the issue and said we would return another day to see if he had changed his mind.

We visited a children's project, where we had UNICEF funding to create a pond in the outdoor space of some tower blocks that housed communities originating from Serbia, Albania, and Yugoslavia, and from various Roma communities that had been living in Kosovo for generations. The idea was that the children would invite their parents to view their pond, gathering there and building peaceful relations. We provided certificates, food, and drinks there in a hot, sultry atmosphere.

One of my first evenings was spent reviewing the project plan with the team and evaluating progress up to that point. We then plotted actions and a way forward. We sat under a cascade of wisteria all evening and were eaten by mosquitos while we drank tea and ate the grapes, cheese, and Swiss chocolate we had brought as gifts for the team. The logistician was so happy to have been given some new direction that he took the flip-chart pages to his room and typed them up overnight!

I spent much of my trip coaching, counselling, and appraising the Medair team. One woman was suffering from PTSD after a previous war-zone project where her car had been rocked and stoned following an accident. I thought she should go home, and she wanted to leave as soon as possible. She was too scared to tell the founder, a medic, so I agreed to speak for her. As the three of us met, the woman did not have the confidence to follow through with her request, and I later received a telling off from the founder. I learned a tough and valuable lesson: never come between people or try to speak on their behalf. It was a typical aid work operation versus HR struggle, and I often lost, as I had compassion for the individual even at the cost of a project, which to me could always wait.

It was hot and airless in the bedroom, and one day I decided to open the window in our small room. The window was over my founder's bed, while my bed was at a right angle to it. There was a piece of paper pasted to the window, written in Albanian, but I didn't think it could be very important. How wrong I was. To anyone able to read Albanian, it was perfectly clear: "DO NOT OPEN THE WINDOW!"

In the middle of the night, the window fell in on my boss with a loud crashing sound! Luckily, the pane didn't break and she was unharmed. This was yet another lesson in war zone work: be prepared for the unexpected and ask questions rather than taking the initiative and making assumptions!

Toward the end of my stay in Kosovo, we returned to the elderly Albanian man to check on his housing. He told us his daughter had taken her own life the day before by hanging herself from a beam in the house. He paused, then said, "You see, I knew I didn't need that roof – now there's only me." I have never been able to get this out of my mind. Perhaps the new roof would have saved her life.

We met some people selling contraband cigarettes and chatted for a while. They said the war in Kosovo would never end, as the atrocities would need to be avenged. One of them said, "There will again be blood on the land, and never peace." I had much to process, and I still wait, hoping and praying that he was wrong.

South Sudan

In 2003-04 I found myself working for Medair in Padak, on the White Nile in South Sudan, and living in a *tukul* – a mud-made animal hut. I had very little materially, yet I remember feeling the happiest I had ever been. There was no electricity or mobile phone, but I had a cumbersome satellite phone for emergencies. My main methods of communication were the letters and cards I had taken with me in my essential 10kg of luggage.

Every few weeks we received a plane delivery of basic tinned food and precious mail. As I walked to my capacity-building teaching job one day, I remember thinking: "If life ever gets too much, I need to remember there is a place where I can be happier." This thought has helped me through many challenges. When life gets tough, I only need to change one thing: where I am, what I am doing, or who I am with.

Some of the challenges in South Sudan were caused by a lack of resources, which were just not as available as in the West. For example, a two-year-old toddler poured a pot of boiling water straight off the fire over himself and ended up with a head wound, which was treated with gentian violet, an antiseptic dye primarily used to treat fungal infections. On another occasion, a mother decided she needed to return home to her husband, her other three children, and her fields rather than staying with her sick child, despite the fact that the child only needed a couple more days in our hospital unit. Her view of the value of life was very different from the Western view, but as a farmer she had observed life and death closely.

Even for us as a team, choices were stark. The frequent drills to prepare for attack gave us the options of a) staying in the compound and being bombed or b) jumping into the open bomb shelter pit, which was inhabited by poisonous snakes! We had a snake pole beside our *tukul* home. My bed was a plank of wood resting on four oil drums, yet I found some fabric and made it into a pink palace with a couple of bed sheets and a plastic chair.

On my way to deliver a lecture in the community hut, I met the chief's armed driver. "Would you like to see my weapon?" he asked. What could I say? I showed a degree of interest in his Kalashnikov, telling him I had served in the Officers' Training Corps for three years while at university. I hoped it was the right answer. He saluted me, and I left rather quickly!

Questions of faith and belief often came up in my classes, and one student in my leadership class asked, "How many moons do you have in your land?" I answered as best I could, adding with a smile that I had "flown like a bird in the sky to reach them".

Five months before heading to South Sudan, I had met a man who wanted to marry me. We wrote weekly while I was overseas, and in one of my letters I shared that I had been offered another assignment in northern Uganda, Sudan, and Kenya. As I wrote – to see if he could imagine serving as a pastor/teacher in Africa with me – he was offered a vicar and wife post in Buckinghamshire. Suddenly, we had options! He decided to turn down the vicar post, but we discerned that he was not well enough to accompany me to Africa, having been admitted to hospital for a defibrillator fitting on Christmas Eve. I felt my calling was too strong to turn down, and he agreed to wait until I retired – yes, retired! Then he sacrificially let me go... So back I went to Africa. Little did I know that this sacrificial letting go was to open up an extraordinary opportunity.

North Sudan and West Darfur

After my six months in South Sudan I headed to North Sudan. My role there was again capacity-building – coaching the country director and senior managers in Khartoum, and training beneficiary leaders of the community across all Medair project sites in North Sudan. These included the heads of civil society: officials in the police, judiciary, education, health, water, and various other sectors. Unlike in South Sudan – where I wore field clothes of trousers and tops – I wanted to mirror the women in our office, so I went to the local market to buy suitable ankle-length skirts, heels, make-up, and jewellery. I also chose to be veiled. Although this was an effort in the forty-degree heat, I was respected by my male students and did not pose a threat to their wives. It also gave me a degree of protection and respect. One female colleague was asked, "Why do you dress like a man rather than a woman, as your sister does?" Each one of us had to choose which elements of a culture to adopt.

I worked in an internally displaced persons (IDP) camp for a while, training local volunteers and staff. Our Sabbath became a Friday, where we attended church when we could. Sometimes it was dangerous, especially for Muslim converts.

All too soon, I headed to the stunning rural Nuba Mountains area and went free climbing on a day off with my tall, leggy team – just managing to keep up and scale the rocks. From there I headed to West Darfur, where civil war was still very much alive.

It was an ordinary day in 2005 when our team was on the road and found Fatima (whom I described in the Introduction) lying in the bush. She was heavily pregnant and we took her to our clinic, where she later received a caesarean section delivery.

At only eleven years old, her pregnancy was the result of conflict rape carried out by the militia. I knew that this was by no means uncommon for girls and young women in rural villages or in IDP camps. The militia or rebels were often given immunity from civil prosecutions, while the police were usually only present in towns and lacked the basic tools or political will to respond to sexual violence. Survivors like Fatima have no meaningful access to redress. They are fearful of the consequences of reporting and lack the resources needed to prosecute their perpetrators. The local Médecins Sans Frontières clinic team reported 500 rapes during the six months I was in West Darfur, with more than 80% taking place while village girls and women were carrying out daily activities, such as collecting water or tending livestock. The rest took place while they were fleeing to neighbouring Chad for safety.

FGM

As Fatima recovered, I began to learn more about the complications that can follow on from FGM. Aged five, Fatima had experienced FGM in a rural context – at the hands of an elder or her own grandmother, probably held down by aunts and watched by her mother. This would likely have led to psychological trauma and flashbacks. Attachment bonds may have been severed as she realized her most trusted relatives had carried out this harmful practice. Fatima's FGM experience may also have replayed in her mind as she was raped by the militia soldiers. Five years later, left for dead and forced to fend for herself, Fatima soon realized she was very vulnerable as an orphaned girl without male protection in rural, war-torn Darfur.

As I headed to Medair's regional base in Nairobi, Kenya, I couldn't help thinking about Fatima and hoping she was safe in her new setting. I kept picturing the words "for such a time as this", and looked up the book of Esther in the Bible. This book was a favourite of mine, since I had practised and later converted to Judaism during my twenties. Esther had been selected for potential forced marriage, yet she used her position to help deliver her people from persecution. In Esther 4:14, her uncle reminds her, "And who knows but that you have come to your royal position for such a time as this?" Perhaps meeting Fatima was my Esther moment, and God would use it to free girls from FGM and the forced marriage that often follows. I had certainly cried out to him for Fatima's safety, asking who would care for these girls and hearing the audible reply, "You will!" No pressure, then!

I was due to take a week's leave with two Medair friends following the wedding of another two of our colleagues. I went to the after-party, while my travelling buddies headed to the office to collect our tickets. It was dark and the office was in a remote area, and their vehicle was carjacked. My male friend had his laptop stolen at gunpoint. My female friend, aged twenty-one, was raped. The assailants could not believe they had no cash, so they took what they could.

Returning from the wedding, the jubilant mood of our team turned to shock and horror. Our holiday was cancelled, and I looked after my colleagues as they faced physical and psychological check-ups before being sent to Scotland for debriefing a week later. Sitting in the rape debrief, I realized I too had been raped during my twenties but had blocked out the memories.

As our luggage was loaded from the curb into the taxi, I tripped over a case in my hallway and hurt my foot. A week later, when I realized my toes were uneven, an X-ray revealed I had broken my foot, so I came home on crutches with my lower leg in a cast.

A change of plan

As I travelled back to the UK, it felt as though circumstances were colluding to direct the future. My new assignment in Darfur was cancelled as the war escalated again, and all non-essential staff were sent out of the country. Despite my having a role, a visa, and a desire to return, it was not to be. Instead, I went to Le Ruchet, France, after a debrief at Medair's Swiss head office. After a week of processing much of my aid work since 2001, and the hurts of life, the secondary trauma of working in Kosovo, northern Uganda, North and South Sudan, and Kenya, I felt more balanced again. I also realized that I shared certain similarities with Fatima, as I had experienced child abuse, rape, and the death of my parents. Other doors were closing, and I felt very clearly that God was leading me to help end FGM.

I spoke to the man who had proposed marriage about this and he proposed again! I kept the silver pledge ring he gave me and always wore it.

I talked to my church leaders, who were less than enthusiastic about my anti-FGM calling, as they were concerned for my physical and emotional wellbeing. Some years later I went to InterHealth for a psychological assessment, and after two and a half hours I was confirmed as fit for any global assignments. I called it my Sanity Certificate and proudly put it up on my wall!

My church leaders suggested that I get a job, knowing I had the ability to earn money as an HR consultant. This did not feel like the right fit with my calling, nor would it have helped me gain experience in FGM in honour of Fatima and the many other girls like her.

As my foot healed, I adjusted to UK life with a fair degree of culture shock, but life settled back into a more restful pattern. The first time I was taken food shopping after returning home, I had a crisis in the jam aisle at Tesco, saying, "I just want a jar of red jam." I was overwhelmed by the hundreds of choices!

My heart also healed, despite the death of my close friends' five-year-old daughter. Facing these challenges and shedding some frozen tears, I committed to undertaking a Healing Prayer School course for holistic healing with Lin Button, and I came to terms with why God could allow sufferings like the death of a child and Fatima's FGM to occur.

Gaining experience

I was completing a PsyD (psychology), partly by correspondence and partly at schools in Hawaii, California, and London. I had chosen an American psychology course, as I wanted it to be relevant to cross-cultural mission work and to add to the UK business studies degree I had taken during my late teens. I decided to dedicate three months to completing all the outstanding work, finishing a year ahead of the deadline in spring 2006.

I also committed to serving at a summer camp for child survivors of cancer in Belarus with Samaritan's Purse in order to experience a different type of Christian organization. I was curious about where I would fit best on the spectrum from overt evangelism (think Billy Graham) to showing faith through acts (more of a chaplaincy role), and on the spectrum from a professional humanitarian agency (like Medair) to a more laid-back volunteer agency (like YWAM). Samaritan's Purse was not for me, as other volunteers there had very different views on orphanages and aid.

I was asked to undertake two pieces of HR consultancy for Tearfund, and I earned a good income for this while also gaining development experience. I was tasked with a five-month assignment to show whether Tearfund's work had made an impact over ten years. It involved working with another consultant for some parts, interviewing partners across the world by telephone or questionnaire, and reading hundreds of files. I also interviewed dozens of staff members at all levels of the organization. The project had been attempted before, but had been a poisoned chalice assignment for an internal staff member.

I was also asked to carry out an evaluation of the regional advisor role to establish whether it was best for this position to be placed in-country or at Tearfund's head office in the UK. I commuted from Barnet to Teddington three days a week, and it felt odd to be back in smart work clothes. The project culminated in me presenting to staff about their future. It wasn't at all easy, yet this allowed me to incorporate any concerns into my final report. With this project ending and my PsyD completed, I was ready for the next challenge. I had saved some funds for overseas trips to Belarus and for a Youth with a Mission (YWAM) school in the USA from September 2006 to February 2007.

The YWAM trip was in a 10/40 window context: the window between ten degrees and forty degrees north latitude that encapsulates some of the most disadvantaged people in the world. I headed off to Colorado Springs, USA, as I had experienced some cross-cultural issues with two US ex-military teams from Medair and wanted to get to know them so I could understand and love them better. I was part of a school of twenty-five: two couples, three children under five, four internationals (a Swedish woman and three British, including myself), and the rest young American women aged between eighteen and twenty-five. We spent three months in a wooden hill lodge, as the usual hotel had burned down in an electric fire. We were in a dormitory of nine, including one young woman who spent her entire pregnancy with us.

We spent our three-month outreach in Thailand, Myanmar, and China doing amazing tasks – including feeding Burmese refugees who had swum across the river to a safe house in Thailand, teaching English to the ministers of wrestling and cycling for the Beijing Olympics, and providing arts and religious education in the form of song and dance to children who had been sponsored through Compassion. I was happy to be involved in all of these, though I performed some tasks better than others. I managed to swallow large dried locusts as food, for example, but only made the back row in the dance concert!

On returning to the UK, I was shocked to be treated as a migrant by the government, and faced numerous challenges to prove my right to reside and work in the UK. I felt I needed to pursue the FGM calling further, having reflected on and prayed about it for the seven months I had been overseas. I looked at various mission and theological colleges offering degrees, and settled on one at All Nations Christian College (ANCC) in

Ware. I was only planning to take the second year, but was told that if I also took the final year I would be awarded a degree. I later chose to take half of the first-year classes alongside my second-year classes, and the remaining half with my third year. This meant I completed all three years in two, paying just two years of fees but benefitting from a grounding in all subjects.

I spent a delightful couple of years at ANCC, commuting daily from Barnet. I was there for the 8.30 a.m. tutor group, had classes all morning, and then enjoyed lunch with classmates, other year groups, MA students, and staff – up to 200 people at any one time. Afternoons were spent studying in the library.

Although all assignments were anonymous, I managed to find an FGM angle for almost all of them, so my assignments were fairly easy to identify! I studied gender, Islam, anthropology, world religions, development, and biblical modules, plus practical modules such as hairdressing, self-defence, car maintenance, and cross-cultural cooking, to prepare me for life overseas. I took on a placement with my church and volunteered at Strawberry Vale Estate in Barnet for a year. I spent my other one-year placement teaching English to Bangladeshi women living in Luton, also teaching citizenship and cultural studies around explanations of Christmas and Easter. Many of the women were very young and had come to Britain to be married to older cousins. They did not know their UK rights with regard to protection against violence in marriage. We provided some with safe houses.

During my summer break, I went to Dadaab on the Kenyan–Somali border and worked as an advisor in the gender-based violence unit, working with Kenyan staff and Somali volunteers. We dealt with cases of FGM, rape, defilement, and violence, and we took clients to hospital, police, court, or specialist services to deal with their abuse. Porous borders meant the country boundaries were often, in reality, lines in the sand. There was a circular wire fence around the camp that housed 250,000 refugees and asylum seekers. Beyond the wire was a five-kilometre circumference, indicating where benefits were still being given to local Kenyans for fuel, schooling, food, medicine, housing, and training to partly compensate for the full funding given to the refugees at the camp. Even so, some Kenyans were said to agree with the local phrase: "You rape our trees [cut for firewood for huts], we'll rape your women." I wondered whether the allowance was enough to appease such feelings.

I was once asked by a judge to suggest an appropriate sentence for a woman who had hit another woman and knocked her teeth out. I suggested some cows were offered to compensate for her lower bride value, based on my Sudanese experience. I was told her marriageability was not at risk as she was still pure and a virgin. The punishment was settled at half a camel.

I spent time calculating how long it would take to communicate with all the 250,000 Somalis at the camp while I was there. There were sixty people who had seen that FGM was not a good thing: village chiefs, religious leaders, men, women, uncut girls, and youth. These sixty represented a precious 0.00024% of the population, but it was a start. If they all taught everything they knew to others, who in turn taught others… This was the same idea British chef Jamie Oliver had for changing the eating habits of a city like Sheffield: train one person, who trains two more, who trains two more, and so on. I predicted the whole camp could be trained in anti-FGM work in around five years.

Back in the UK, I signed up for a two-year internship at Forward, an African women's diaspora charity near Wormwood Scrubs. Naana, the CEO, had another intern, Julia, who won a competition to go to the World Economic Forum in Davos, and went on to set up her own charity, Orchid Project, to work toward ending female genital cutting. Julia launched her charity a year ahead of mine. Forward was not interested in supporting my charity idea, so during my internship I did some research behind the scenes to train and equip myself. I was able to take a counselling course at the Women & Girls Network to support survivors of violence against women. This one-year course also taught me about violence, forced marriage, FGM, and other related issues, such as rape, poverty, and embryonic gender selection.

I worked on Forward's Sierra Leone project from the UK, which aimed to support child mothers and vulnerable girls in marginalized communities in Freetown Sierra Leone. I had planned to visit, but Ebola struck, so this was not possible. I also worked in UK schools, and attended and helped at various film events on witchcraft, FGM, and related topics. I enrolled on an FGM module at King's College, but the course was cancelled because only seven people registered, so I arranged some training myself. This involved meeting DCI Allan Davies from the Metropolitan Police and Juliet Albert, an FGM specialist midwife at Imperial College Healthcare NHS Trust. I accompanied Juliet and received specialist training from her.

It was very moving to hear about FGM from frontline professionals, and to hear the reasons why young women wanted deinfibulation. Enduring this painful and intrusive procedure was necessary to physically enable sexual relations and subsequent childbirth. One young woman I helped – dressed from head to toe in black – was engaged and intended to consummate her marriage. Her fiancé was a doctor and had sent her, chaperoned by an elderly relative, to be deinfibulated prior to marriage. I worried about all the girls and women affected by FGM who wouldn't know what was needed before marriage. I thought of the women in Darfur who could not sit down for a week after they were married.

Pakistan

While I was at Forward, I took the opportunity to spend four months in northern Pakistan, shadowing and studying under a retiring midwife tutor. She was heading back there for one last trip to oversee exams and check on lesson materials. We were joined by another retired nurse midwife from the UK.

Having faced immense problems getting a visa, including three trips to the embassy, I flew to Islamabad and was driven the length of the country in an old Land Rover. I knew this would be the most dangerous part of the trip, as two women could easily be taken – for the car and themselves – by soldiers travelling across the border from Afghanistan. The roads were also treacherous, with deep chasms on either side. Landslides and mud falls were frequent, and no one wore a seat belt. There were many trucks at the bottom of the ravines, and the hospital orthopaedic wards were full of semi-comatose patients who had been injured in accidents. I went to pray for some of them later in my stay. I was covered from head to toe, wearing a pyjama-like *salwar kameez* suit, but also wrapped in a bed sheet of purple, white, and green flowers. The price of safety sometimes involves letting go of elegance!

I was billeted with the hospital administrator while the midwife tutor and midwife shared another flat. We had a prayer meeting each morning and devotions for the young women students each night. They were there doing two years as nurses and then two more as midwives. By their fourth year, all of these rural Muslim women had become Christians. After devotions, we watched Indian movies with chai and cookies before bed. It was a simple, fun life.

I joined the students on the midwifery ward each morning. I also followed the 1,500 pages of Marshall and Raynor's *Myles Textbook for Midwives* that I had taken with me and read daily in order to complete it while I was there. I watched obstetrics videos when we had internet signal, and in the afternoons worked on practicals, such as blood pressure monitoring, bed pans, suppositories in labour, and measuring and estimating term. I also attended women in outpatients and often worked on the antenatal ward, following patients through all stages of labour.

I remember a very short woman who needed a caesarean section. There was no blood available from the family, and the only blood for sale was believed to have been taken from intravenous drug users. Her relatives were all wailing. I offered a pint – after all, I had given nearly seventy pints in the UK and a few more in Africa before this. My offer was translated and they wailed even more! I was confused. It seemed they were very grateful, so off I went to give. As I recovered with a bottle of fizzy soda, I was given a piece of paper to say that I was not HIV positive. Very reassuring!

I remember the first baby I delivered there. I had observed eighteen births by then, and my tutor said, "Sister Ann-Marie, the next lady is yours!" At that moment, a woman came in – who, as was the custom, had travelled down the mountain in a wheelbarrow. She was helped onto the table. I took off my headscarf and tied my green plastic apron over my cream *salwar kameez*. She looked at me and I smiled at her. She had no idea that I had never done this before – but then she had never done it either – so we worked together. The other midwives in my class stood behind me, no doubt wondering whether they would need to catch the baby for me. Out came the child! I felt that if I held on to his ankle he wouldn't fly out! I felt so proud of this little boy, almost as if he were my own child.

As I helped deliver another five babies, I felt my biological function was complete. I also helped in surgery with the caesarean sections, amazed at how many layers down the babies were. I also had to deal with a stillbirth, and was told to "bag it". I decided to treat this baby with the dignity I would have given a live birth. I wrapped him in a muslin and took him to the mother and grandmother. There was a lot of stigma about stillbirth in Pakistan, with many believing stillborn babies were monsters, so I wanted them to see that this baby was perfect, and that the mother would go on to have other perfect babies. I later wrapped him for burial, praying him on his way.

On another occasion I helped deliver a baby with hydrocephalus, who was born pre-term. I had helped deliver a baby in Nigeria who had suffocated in the womb, as the mother was very young and the surgeons couldn't get the baby out. They wanted to cut the hydrocephalus baby's limbs off, but using my midwifery knowledge I urged them to turn the baby to get him out. I gave him resuscitation, but we lost him after thirty minutes, as we had no ventilator. It was so sad that a lack of resources led to this loss of life. Meanwhile, a friend back home had her baby in special care. We prayed for her from Pakistan.

Nigeria

Forward was hoping to receive some funding for a fistula rehabilitation project in Kano State, north-west Nigeria, and it was decided that I would travel there to train the new project manager and her team of office, finance, and logistics managers. I spent all day flying to Abuja in Nigeria via Addis Ababa, Ethiopia, and then on to Kano. I landed late in the evening, and thankfully there was a taxi to meet me. I felt hot and tired, and was sweating in my modest Western clothing. It wasn't until later that I realized the driver was also the logistics manager!

My boss for this project was CEO of the Nigeria organization, a sort of daughter organization to the UK project, where I had been an intern for the previous year. I was staying at the CEO's brother's house, and the door was opened by two young girls of around ten and twelve years old. They insisted on cooking me a full roast chicken dinner from scratch – with vegetables, bread, fruit, and side dishes – when all I really wanted was a shower and sleep! Even at that time it was over thirty degrees. After dinner, and having half unpacked, I eventually fell sleep, despite the hum of the ceiling fan. All too soon it was dawn, and all sorts of sounds of exotic birds, cockerels, donkeys, animals, and insects could be heard.

After a breakfast of eggs on toast, I was surprised to hear that our journey to the project would take a further two and a half hours from Kano. I wondered just how large this city could be. We stopped at a supermarket and I was told to buy food. I didn't know how long for, and I didn't want to appear colonial and rich, so I just bought some basics: a box of fruit and fibre cereal, a jar of apricot jam, a jar of salad cream, a packet of pasta, a few tins of tuna, tomatoes, teabags, water, and eggs. I guessed I should buy enough for a week, and was told I could buy bread locally later. Little did I know that I wouldn't see a supermarket again in the five months I was there!

On we journeyed, and we eventually arrived at lunchtime. There we met the CEO's nineteen-year-old nephew, Gabriel, who seemed to work on the farm project and often lived in the house. Everyone who came to meet the CEO knelt on the floor to greet her.

Having met the staff, I was given a tour of the site. The office was a double-gated compound with a carport inside and two staircases leading up to a first-floor office on the left and an apartment on the right. Each unit had a reception or lounge area, a small bedroom or manager's office, a double bedroom or double office, a kitchen, and a bathroom.

With no air conditioning and the electricity supplied only via the office generator from 9 a.m. to 4 p.m., I really felt the heat. It was nearly forty degrees, as this northern part of Kano State is on the edge of the Niger desert. To my great surprise, the CEO was heading to the UK on the Monday – in two days' time – and would not be returning until my time in Nigeria was over! I went to unpack in the small bedroom with a single bed and one tap for a shower. There was no mosquito net and my possessions looked quite meagre, yet it already felt like home. I had a short siesta, then rejoined the CEO and Gabriel, who was to be my chaperone. I was to move into her room the next day, and he was to move into mine. The good thing was that the kitchen and bathroom were near my bedroom, and were accessed by another locked door. By custom, Nigerian men could not access the kitchen, so I felt these were my quarters. The nephew was to be fed by other people's mothers.

That evening, we were "entertained" by a semi-pornographic Indian movie in which a woman was dragged through the jungle by her hair, dressed only in a bikini. I suggested he change the channel, but was firmly told by his aunt that it was harmless and to leave him alone. I felt this portrayal of women did not bode well for our future flat-sharing arrangement! I felt disturbed by the images and soon retired to bed.

I told the CEO that I needed a briefing before she left. She suggested I accompany her on her Sunday visits so we could talk on the way. The first stop was with her brother, , who I later learned was chair of the Nigerian NGO. Not good governance practice, I reflected. Little did I know that he was also head of the Islamic State Court in Kano. The house was segregated, with men at the front and women at the back, which provided an insight into another world. My first cultural faux pas was the offer of my hand to greet him after my boss had kissed him on both cheeks. She slapped my hand hard, making a loud noise in the silence.

As we left the house she said, through gritted teeth, "Did you have to offer your hand to the head of the Islamic court?" I would not have done so if I had known, of course, yet I had simply been told that he was her brother. I kept silent, aside from offering an apology, though I felt the injustice of not having been properly briefed and told the correct etiquette. My hand bore a red stripe as we headed to our next meeting.

Keen not to make a similar mistake again, I copied exactly what she did from that point on. We went to meet the head of the local town – the city mayor, who was of royal lineage –and were shown into a large, empty, dusty room. In the far corner was a small door and a chair on a dais. As the mayor entered, wearing a shabby, floor-length shirt, loose trousers, and flip-flops, we dropped to our knees. I followed my host, a foot from her backside, crawling across the sandy floor and keeping my eyes down. I struggled not to giggle out of nervousness, feeling like a small animal following its mother. After greetings and much curtseying, we were done. I was given permission to work in the town, and off we set again in the car, driven by the logistics manager. We discussed my project tasks, and I felt I was all set for my five-month assignment. As the CEO went home to pack, I considered my project goals and reflected on my first day in the office.

Monday dawned, and I was introduced to the team of four managers before being given a tour of the site, the school, the girls' dorms, and the classroom. I decided to eat with the girls. It was homemade couscous, served in a large black cauldron over an open fire, with yoghurt for desert. I added the latter to the former, as it was otherwise too dry to swallow in forty-degree heat. The manager was amazed that I wanted to eat with the girls and sit on the floor mats with them. She sat on a chair away to one side, anxious about the smell of urine. All the girls had fistulae (tears), incontinence from child marriage, and/or FGM. Each carried a bucket.

I later asked where the meat was, as it was supposedly good for body restoration prior to fistula surgery. I was told it was shredded, so that was why I couldn't taste it. I smiled. As a lifelong vegetarian, I knew there was no meat in the dish. It reminded me of the story of the emperor's new clothes. I felt I was steadily gathering questions, but I was unsure how to get them answered truthfully.

I had moved into the CEO's bedroom by this point, where there was a plastic air mattress with a single sheet on it. It was a sweat bath in forty-degree heat, day and night, and within a week my chest looked as though I had the pox. Calamine lotion and baby oil eventually sorted my infected skin out! There was only enough electricity to work the office machines in the daytime and keep the staff cool. From 4 p.m. to 9 p.m. it was unbearably hot, with no access to fans. I only had a head torch for a lamp and a Primus stove to cook with.

Gabriel was offered an upgrade to the room I had vacated, which had a shower in one corner. Unfortunately, he seemed to think I came free with the accommodation and made various passes at me, all uncomfortable and awkward. What's more, he had to escort me to the market weekly to buy rotting tomatoes, okra, or onions, individual eggs, and an occasional jar of tomato paste or a tin of sardines (which I kept in the freezer compartment of the refrigerator at night). Despite being kept in the fridge, bananas and bread quickly turned black or mouldy, but with apricot jam or salad cream I could make some sort of sandwich and eat it with a packet soup or cup of Milo (a chocolate drink). Dinner was locally grown gritty rice, pasta, or couscous with any boiled vegetables I could find, along with egg, tuna, or sardines for protein.

My role was to help the team prepare for a new grant from a UK funding source. The project had previously been a recipient of the Big Lottery Fund, but was to be funded by the Islamic

Development Bank. The project had fallen behind with a change of manager, and the new one was not trained in these skills. She spent her day playing Solitaire on the office computer, had her car washed daily by the logistics team, ordered in food for lunch, and left an hour early because she had "worked through lunch"! I learned that there were no job descriptions, appraisals, policies, or project plans, and very little was functioning from a business perspective. There were no school curriculums, timetables, meetings for teachers, or attendance registers. All this needed to be put in place before the project was ready for UK funding.

It appeared as though the Islamic Development Bank only wanted photos of happy, smiling children as proof of project outcomes. My development studies tutor would have held up his hands in horror! I decided to teach project management by drawing a huge Gantt chart the size of eight flip-chart sheets, which I nailed to the office wall. We tracked all the work completed, not completed, and any extra work completed that had not been requested. I scared them by saying that the donor might ask for the money back if objectives remained unmet, and their salaries could be stopped. That got their attention!

The evenings were quiet, as I usually finished work at 5 p.m., an hour after the staff had left. My only "cool" moments in the day came from lying in a couple of bowls of bath water. As I wore local fabric outfits, the bath water often turned orange, purple, or turquoise from the dye.

As time progressed, so did the challenges. One Saturday I was asked to approve a re-roofing project. I was expected to just sign a payment chit, but I said I wouldn't do so until I had inspected the work, so we all walked out of the office compound. I needed to inspect the roof, and I said that I would follow the others up the stepladder to protect my modesty. They were amazed to see me up there with the logistics manager and supplier, saying, "Hausa women don't climb ladders!" I explained I was not Hausa (the ethnic group in that part of Nigeria), and that I needed to inspect the project to ensure it had been completed as specified by the logistics manager. Rule number one of project development demonstrated!

One of my other aims was to clear out the cupboards, one of which was locked with no evidence of a key. I asked a handyman to break open the padlock and found more than 100 birthing kits that had been donated by Nigeria's first lady. She would not have been pleased if she had known. I decided to give them out quickly, as the rubber suction tubes were starting to perish. We sorted hundreds of posters into fifteen sets and planned a village distribution, along with the birthing kits. This was great for the villages that were staffed by traditional birth attendants, and we also taught on anti-FGM, breastfeeding, reproductive health, and good nutrition.

I started using my Sundays to volunteer at the local hospital, and was pleased to help out in the delivery suite. I helped four women bring their babies into the world. In addition to the six babies I had helped deliver in Pakistan earlier that year, I was proud to have contributed to the arrival of ten new lives. As a childless, single woman – once married, but divorced for more than twenty years – I also felt fulfilled.

There is a definite cultural divide between what a girl or woman can do in Nigerian culture compared with a boy or man. The boys, including Gabriel, played football most evenings, often kicking the ball over my twenty-foot-high compound wall. These young men – aged nineteen to twenty-five – were tall, lanky, and fit, and acted like a pack. On a few occasions I had thrown the ball back over the fence as I sat reading on a tree stump from 5.30 to 6 p.m., prior to making dinner while it was still light and then retiring to bed. I only had two books with me, and had read one and a half during my first week, so I divided the remaining half book by the number of nights left of my stay, leaving me with two pages to read each day. As this did not take long, I wrote a journal from birth to 2010, only to lose it somewhere in the house, having hidden it so well!

I was bathing one day when a knock came on the outer door of the compound. Jumping out of the bath, I covered myself up and edged toward the living room window. I had done this before, so I knew to wind the curtains around my head before leaning out to say that my chaperone would be back later.

As I entered the sitting room, I was shocked and frightened to discover an unwelcome visitor standing in front of me. I could hardly believe this, as it was forbidden to have a man in the house of an unchaperoned woman. Also, he had somehow made it though the compound gate (solid metal double doors) and the front door. The only way was with two separate keys. I quickly assessed my options, knowing that if I was seen I could be arrested for "tempting a man to rape", and imprisoned or stoned to death under Sharia law. In Sudan, women would have been kept underground in a pit until they died.

I instinctively shouted, "Who are you? What are you doing here?" quickly followed by, "Get out of my house. Shoo!" Then I quickly returned to my bedroom and slammed the door. Feeling shaken by this intrusion of my privacy and threat to my safety, I quickly dressed and went down to the front compound door to bolt it from the inside.

When my chaperone returned, he couldn't get in with his key, so I went out to meet him and unbolted the door. I explained how angry I was about what had happened. His only comment was, "Oh God, this is very bad." I said I wanted an identity parade of all the men in the town. This never happened, of course, but it made the point that I was serious, and that I would take steps to protect myself.

A few days later I heard the clink of the compound lock and eight to ten football youths burst in. My body froze, yet somehow I managed to get to my feet and down to the compound door to refuse them entry, pushing them back outside. I threw the ball over the fence and went back inside, with my heart beating very quickly. When my chaperone returned home later, he said they hadn't liked the fact that I was angry. I tried to explain the safety implications of the situation, but he failed to see it from a woman's perspective.

Wearing a red Stetson and adopting a big swagger, he was very jocular as we walked into town that Sunday to buy food, He said, "Gabriel now has his Miriam", using our Arabic names. He also said, "Your breasts are very small, so you look young, but you are old." I told him not to speak to me like that.

Once he walked through the apartment with dirty football boots on just after I had swept the floor following a dust storm. I told him to take off his boots and re-sweep the floor. He refused, yet, having defied me as his elder, I ordered him to "Get on your knees!" To my amazement, he did! I said he must not disrespect me. My only sanctuary was the kitchen, to which he was denied access. I never felt safe, and I started ticking off the number of days I had left on this most challenging of overseas projects.

It proved difficult to transform the project in the five months I had there, as there was no culture of attendance from the young women in the six-month rehabilitation programme or from the tertiary college teachers. There were plenty of cultural challenges, too, for example I was told not to sweep up bits of an Arabic textbook, as it was part of the Qur'an and must not be thrown away. I produced timetables, register contracts, and codes of practice, but the forty-degree heat led to general apathy and disinterest in my work. Change was not usually welcomed in rural Nigeria.

I became aware of a double set of accounts, presumably shown to auditors, yet I wondered what I was supposed to do with this information. There were many discrepancies in the accounts and annual reports. The early question, "Where is the meat for the restorative health diet?" was a good example of the lack of transparency I came up against. Another was, "Where is the project motorbike?" Answers included, "It was in an accident" and "It is at a staff member's house". I started going through all the accounts at night, and borrowed files from the office once I was alone. I could see clear irregularities and was told various stories by whistle-blowers. I jotted it all down in my notebook.

I was planning on travelling to the south of Nigeria with the accountant, who was a Christian, for a weekend visit. However, the CEO called from the UK just as we were about to leave. She forbade me to travel, saying the police knew where I was and that it would be a great shame if I were to have an accident. "The last person who travelled without approval ended up in a police cell," she said, "and although she wasn't raped, she was lucky." I was upset and angry, yet I had no choice. There was no opportunity to go to church or to see the middle part of Nigeria, and there was no holiday. I unpacked and regrouped.

The longer I was there, the more I found out about the corruption taking place. I received several direct death threats from the project manager as a result. Luckily for me, the office manager's ethnic group, or "tribe", as she called it, was from a different state. She warned me that my life was in danger and that the project manager's son had agreed to get rid of me for a handful of dollars. Having already had the difficult experience of a random stranger turning up in my apartment through two locked doors and the football team bursting into my compound, I knew men could easily pass through locked doors using keys that had presumably been made available for a price.

I also had to survive the wildlife, which included snakes and scorpions. On one occasion, a plague of flying insects dropped all their wings on the wall of the house under the outdoor light on the same day. It was absolutely covered! I also felt violated by a very opportunistic cockroach that crept under the mattress and got inside my mosquito net – only to be found sitting on my hip! I wondered, in horror and revulsion, how long it had circled over my sweaty body. There had been no mosquito net when I arrived, and I had complained endlessly that this was the only place I had been where one had not been provided. A net eventually appeared, but I had to do some creative Heath Robinson construction to keep it in the air – making strings from elastic bands and opened-out paperclips tied onto the door handle and curtain pole!

When two generators broke, I was accused of breaking them, owing to overuse. Ironically, I had no control over either, and no one used them after the office closed at 4 p.m. as the staff supposedly worked through their lunch breaks so they could leave an hour early. This meant I didn't even have oil, electricity, or cool air, and there was no way of cooking proper meals. I resorted to boiling a large pan of water on a camping stove with my head torch on. I put rotting okra, onions, or tomatoes in the base with the pasta, rice, or couscous. I put a cup of Milo in the middle to warm up. On the top I put a plate to warm tuna or cook an egg, with another bowl on top containing mashed banana for pudding. The pile of plates rattled precariously in the dark, lit only by the blue glow of gas and my head torch. I smiled at my resilience, but with only enough gas for two more days I knew I had to speak to someone about my dire living conditions.

I asked my office manager to arrange for me to meet two of the trustees, and took a car there. They were embarrassed to hear about my situation, and after feeding me they took me to a supermarket to buy pasta, fruit, eggs, and vegetables, refusing all offers of payment. I felt much better after meeting these two women. I cautiously hinted at some of my concerns on the state of the project, as I was wary that the chair of the board was the CEO's brother, and I wasn't sure how far up the organization the poor governance went.

That night there was a huge dust storm, accompanied by a very loud roar from across Niger. I genuinely thought I might die, as the sound was so deathly and terrifying!

Once I returned to the UK, I spoke to the CEO of the parent charity, as I felt sure she would want to pass these comments on to potential funders. The project needed a root and branch overhaul before it would be fit to support and fund. She listened for a couple of hours before saying, "You're tougher than we imagined." I always wondered what that meant. Apparently, all previous visitors had stayed in a city hotel and made one short visit to the project.

A couple of weeks later I was asked to meet the CEO of the Nigerian organization. She and her sons were British and had homes in London. I could not keep to myself all that had been whistle-blown to me, and what I had found out from my own investigations, but I was concerned that it would all come back to haunt me. Unlike all my other overseas trips, I had been totally alone there. The project eventually closed and justice was meted out.

I felt unsafe for six months, waiting to be attacked or killed. A couple of months later I sought counselling to help me process the trauma of this trip. Sitting on top of years of other war-zone experiences, I needed a safe way to process and park it.

THREE:
WHAT IS FGM?

This chapter draws on my academic paper in the *Journal of Gender Studies*,[2] case studies about my experience in the field, and various 28 Too Many research reports explaining the reasons for, consequences of, and prevalence of FGM across twenty-eight African countries. It includes insights gathered from twenty years of working in Africa and from 28 Too Many's "Social Norms and FGM" report.[3]

The World Health Organization (WHO) defines FGM as:

> **All procedures that involve partial or total removal of the external female genitalia, or other injury to the female genital organs for non-medical reasons... It reflects deep-rooted inequality between the sexes, and constitutes an extreme form of discrimination against women. It is nearly always carried out on minors and is a violation of the rights of children. The practice also violates a person's rights to health, security and physical integrity, the right to be free from torture and cruel, inhuman or degrading treatment, and the right to life when the procedure results in death.[4]**

---

2   www.tandfonline.com/doi/full/10.1080/09589236.2012.681182.
3   www.28toomany.org/thematic/social-norms-and-fgm.
4   www.who.int/news-room/fact-sheets/detail/female-genital-mutilation.

There are four main types of FGM:

- **Type I** is referred to as clitoridectomy and involves the partial or total removal of the external clitoris and/or the prepuce (the fold of skin surrounding the clitoris).
- **Type II** (or excision) is the partial or total removal of both the external clitoris and the labia minora (the inner folds of the vulva). This can, but doesn't always, include the excision of the labia majora (the outer folds of the vulva).
- **Type III** (or infibulation) involves the narrowing of the vaginal orifice with the creation of a covering seal. This is done by cutting and repositioning the labia minora and/or labia majora, and can be done with or without excision of the clitoris.
- **Type IV** includes any other harmful procedures to the female genitalia for non-medical purposes, such as pricking, piercing, incising, scraping, and cauterization. Type IV varies in practice between different countries, including those where FGM is not recognized as being prevalent. For example, labia stretching/elongation is a form of Type IV in Southern Africa and includes elongating the labia minora through manual manipulation, such as pulling or the use of physical equipment, such as weights and other objects. Another is the act of scraping the tissue surrounding the vagina (angurya cuts performed in Nigeria), cauterization of the clitoris, and the introduction of corrosive herbs into the vagina to cause bleeding and narrowing.

FGM is an ancient traditional practice that has been taking place for more than 2,000 years. While it is not known exactly where and why it first happened, it is thought to originate from Sudan or Egypt, countries that still have a prevalence rate of over 80%. Egyptian mummies in the British Museum show women were infibulated, with some commentators believing the practice originated there. This is why it is sometimes called pharaonic circumcision. Others believe it first existed among equatorial African herders as a form of protection against rape for young female herders. The custom may also have been an outgrowth of human sacrificial practices or an attempt at population control. In 1609, João dos Santos – a Portuguese missionary to Africa – reported that a group near Mogadishu, Somalia, sewed up their women and especially slaves, who could be sold for more money if chaste. Egyptians practised FGM to prevent pregnancy in female slaves, calling it Sudanese circumcision. It is believed the practice arose independently among different peoples. FGM was newly adopted in some countries as recently as the 1980s, so the geographical presence is both decreasing and increasing.

Often when people think of FGM, they think of the immediate medical consequences of the practice: the physical trauma of the cutting, whether ritualized or in a medical setting; the healing process; and the risk of infection that comes with any surgery. There are, however, many other implications throughout the woman's life, including effects on her mental well-being having been through a traumatic procedure, often at the hands or behest of her closest family members; ongoing health issues resulting from the cutting; and social implications from being subjected to, or not being subjected to, FGM.

It is estimated that at least 200 million women and girls are currently living with the consequences of this practice. It is carried out on females of various ages, from newborns to women who are about to be married. FGM is prevalent in at least twenty-eight countries, mainly in Africa, but also in the Middle East, Asia, and among some ethnic groups in Central and South America. Yet, owing to global migration and the resettling of various groups, it is also increasingly prevalent in diasporic communities across the world in which traditional practices are continued.

Hawa's story

The singular experience for these girls and women is so severe that it can often only be illustrated in their own words. This is how Hawa told me her story:

I was born in 1983 in a village near Jamaame [in Somalia]. I indelibly recall the day when this awful and humiliating practice was done to me. I slept peacefully, yet suspicion crept in as my poor, ignorant mother woke me at dawn, served me milk and led me to bushes on the village outskirts. After some minutes, the great village midwife and retinue appeared. We concluded the occasion's purpose: circumcision!

Soon the atrocious practice started. We were helpless as we followed in succession into the shaking hands of the old woman. She used sharp new razor blades called cutters. I could not save myself; I was only five years old. When my time came, she had a hidden grudge and painfully cut almost all my external genitals. I remember an explosion of hot searing pain in my crotch, as I screamed like a trapped mouse. She sewed the labia after the operation and tied my legs together. A lot of blood oozed out from there, such that I fainted.

When I regained consciousness, all the outer parts of my genitals were cut off and stitched up with thorns, leaving a passage the size of a rice grain. There was still hot pain between my legs and the slightest movement so aggravated it that tears would well up. I used to walk like a grandma because I could move my legs only from the knees down. To reduce the pain of urine pushing through the raw wound of the narrow opening, warm water was poured over it while I urinated. As a result of the fearsome incident, I took shock and in the night got frightened.

Ten years after, I felt the effects of FGM in full swing. I felt kidney problems and got very painful periods since the debris had no place to pass and I contracted infections. This resulted in discontinuation of my classes after collapsing regularly in school. However, more dreadful is what the future holds for me. Seeing the problems of women during delivery and labour, I fear more than ever to marry a man.

Consequences of FGM

As an organization, 28 Too Many refers to the practice as female genital mutilation (FGM), based on the WHO definition. Some non-governmental organizations refer to the practice as female genital cutting (FGC). Our charity believes this description does not adequately explain the significance of the practice, with the word "cutting" minimizing the medical and further implications. The word "mutilation" demonstrates that the practice is an injury, as there are no medical benefits from the practice in any of its forms. It is a violation of the human rights of girls and women. The exception we make in our research and reports is to use the local terminology of the region to avoid alienating communities the charity works alongside.

In the vast majority of cases, women and girls experiencing FGM immediately suffer from severe blood loss, excruciating pain, and shock. Many have no form of anaesthesia, and traditional or risky cutting methods are often employed, such as thorns, fingernails, or rusty blades, resulting in terrible wounds that are difficult to heal, and leading to increased risk of infection and HIV. The procedure is traumatic, violent, and often performed by someone without medical training (the practitioner is a medically trained professional in less than 1% of cases). It is typically carried out by traditional practitioners, who are generally older women. Being a traditional practitioner gives these women status within the community, and they are often paid to carry out the practice, which shows how highly people regard its importance.

The risk of infection is particularly high in the days and weeks after the procedure. Open wounds and stitched orifices present difficulties when it comes to urinating or menstruating, as well as increased risk of bladder infection. It is estimated that girls in education who have experienced FGM also miss out on 25% of their classes, owing to the time it takes to pass urine through the tiny hole left by the procedure. Many women have also experienced alarming infections as a result of menstrual blood being retained in the body.

Many women face multiple and ongoing sexual health issues. With the most extreme types of FGM, the women need to be cut again to enable intercourse, and many experience pain during sex. There are increased incidences of complications and sometimes death in pregnancy and childbirth, and incontinence due to fistulae in the bladder or rectum. Relationships with partners become tense as women can fear sexual intercourse or feel undesirable because of the scarring and other problems. In communities where marriage and offspring are key, women who are unable to fulfil these expectations may experience social exclusion and deep shame. There is an increased likelihood of post-traumatic stress disorder (PTSD), anxiety, and depression. Another common practice that can occur after pregnancy is reinfibulation. This is the act of re-sewing the genitalia after childbirth. The woman is often left with scar tissue around the area after the initial procedure and each childbirth, which can be very painful.

A young woman called Mariam shared her experience with us of becoming pregnant after having FGM. She was married at sixteen and immediately became pregnant. No one had told her about the complications that might occur, and there was no medical assistance for her. She was in labour for four days before she was taken to a regional hospital, where the baby was delivered stillborn. Mariam developed a fistula and was leaking urine, at which point her husband and family completely abandoned her.

Reasons for FGM practice

A large part of the challenge in tackling FGM relates to the diverse reasons it is practised and the variety of communities in which it is prevalent. The reasons communities give for practising FGM include: religious beliefs; maintaining a woman's virginity or chastity; cultural tradition; hygiene; improving female fertility; and increased sexual pleasure for men. FGM is also seen as a rite of passage, making the girl into a woman by removing parts of the genitalia that resemble male parts or are considered more masculine.

FGM is often believed to be a religious requirement. Although it has been found among Islamic, Christian, and (previously) Jewish communities, none of the holy texts of these religions prescribes FGM, and the practice predates Christianity and Islam. The views of religious leaders within these communities vary. Those who support the practice tend to consider FGM a religious act, and the idea of eliminating it to be a threat to their culture and religion. However, there are religious leaders who are willing to support and contribute to efforts to eliminate FGM.

The main reason for FGM is a desire to achieve social approval and acceptance, while simultaneously avoiding disapproval and social sanctions. The practice is referred to as a "social norm". One of the many social factors is preparing a young girl, often as young as ten, for marriage. These girls have a high price to pay if they depart from social norms, particularly in communities where great importance is placed on the dual roles of mother and wife. This is reinforced in communities where it is hard for women to become socially and financially independent owing to a lack of economic opportunities. The prevalence of these social norms also presents challenges for families in these communities, as they risk social exclusion and stigma if they do not have FGM, and their daughters are unable to find a marriage partner.

For change to be enduring, it must be endorsed by the whole community. This is because families are more likely to subject their daughters to the practice if they believe others in their social group expect them to do so. Families can also be encouraged to abandon the practice if they know that the majority of people in their community will follow suit.

Prevalence of FGM

Our charity began its work focusing on the twenty-eight African countries where FGM is most prevalent, although the practice varies greatly across these countries. Mali has a prevalence rate of 89%, which is among the highest, while bordering Mauritania has a rate of 69% and Niger a rate of 2%, which is among the lowest.[5] This variation shows that the diffusion of the practice is influenced more by ethnicity and population group than by nationality. FGM prevalence also varies significantly within each country. It is a cultural practice that is particular to specific ethnic groups, even when they are spread across country borders. For example, Somali communities practise FGM in Somalia and in north-eastern Kenya, while the Maasai community practises FGM in Kenya and Tanzania.

In Burkina Faso, where 76% of women and girls have experienced FGM, it is practised mainly on infants and young girls, with 90.8% cut before the age of ten.[6] Data from a Demographic and Health Study (DHS) showed that 76.8% of women reported being cut with flesh removed.[7] This is the most common type reported among women aged fifteen to forty-nine, with 16.6% reporting being cut with no flesh removed, and only 1.2% reporting Type III/infibulation.

In Burkina Faso, girls born to poorer families in rural areas with no education are the most likely to be cut. Although the overall prevalence of FGM in Nigeria is among the lowest of the African countries (24.8%), studies show that the prevalence is highest within communities of girls born into rich, Christian, urban families. It has also been shown that a mother's level of education is a determining factor in whether her daughters are cut. The typical expectation is that a higher level of education will be linked to a lower likelihood of FGM. However, Nigerian women aged fifteen to forty-nine with no education are notably less likely to have undergone FGM (17.2%) than those with primary-level, secondary-level, or higher education (about 30%). This shows how differently the practice is regarded between countries, and why tailored strategies are needed to abolish it.

---

5   www.28toomany.org/country/niger; www.28toomany.org/country/mauritania.

6   www.28toomany.org/country/burkina-faso.

7   https://dhsprogram.com/pubs/pdf/cr33/cr33.pdf.

In 1996, Burkina Faso was the first African country to introduce a national law that prohibited FGM. A survey of women and girls aged fifteen to forty-nine found that the main reason given for the practice was community or social acceptance. The pressure to continue the practice also comes partly from religious interpretation, as the practice of FGM appears in all religions in Burkina Faso. Despite not being mandated by any religious text, of those aged fifteen to forty-nine who have heard of FGM, 17.3% of women and 14.9% of men believe it is required by their religion – primarily those practising traditional/animist beliefs and Islam. Despite these prevalent social norms, 87.4% of women aged fifteen to forty-nine who have had FGM subsequently believe it should be stopped, while only 11.7% are in favour of its continuation, with 0.8% unsure. The highest level of support for continuation comes from women aged forty-five to forty-nine (11.7%) and men aged fifteen to nineteen (12.2%), which suggests that the importance of these social norms varies between different demographics.

Somalia has one of the highest FGM prevalence rates in the world among women aged fifteen to forty-nine at approximately 98%.[8] It is also highly prevalent within the Somalian diaspora. This is partly because the majority of women moving from Somalia have experienced FGM. Also, many young girls born within Somalian communities in another country are taken to Somalia to have the procedure done. Those who have experienced FGM in Somalian communities usually have the procedure at a young age (typically between ten and fourteen).

Information regarding the prevalence of the different types of FGM in Somalia is difficult to obtain, as recording this information becomes harder when there is variation in definition and interpretation between different communities. FGM is commonly referred to as pharaonic, which is Type III (infibulation), or *sunna*, which many believe to be sanctioned by Islam. However, significant variations in the type of FGM classified as *sunna* exist across Somalia, from pricking of the

8   www.28toomany.org/country/somalia.

clitoris through to more extreme forms that still involve cutting and stitching.

The effort to eliminate this practice in Somalia has been particularly difficult. There is currently no national legislation that expressly criminalizes and punishes the practice, and no penalties have been set out for the practice or procurement of FGM. Recent studies found that 64.5% of women aged fifteen to forty-nine who had heard of FGM believed the practice should continue. As the majority of women condone it, this explains why the practice has been harder to eradicate in Somalia.

While it is generally women who make decisions regarding FGM in Somalia, men and boys are "influential in creating the social climate within which decision-making about it takes place", according to global education, research, and training consultant Katy Newell-Jones.[9] Only 4% of unmarried men surveyed would prefer to marry a girl who has not undergone FGM. Several studies and anecdotal reports note that there is a lack of communication between men and women on the subject in general, and more specifically on the types of cutting, which leads to confusion about what men actually want for their wives and daughters. When led by community activists, discussions with men that begin with human rights and progress to the health impacts of FGM have proved successful in changing attitudes within Somalia. As in Burkina Faso, FGM in Somalia is performed primarily by traditional practitioners, although medicalized FGM (carried out by a health professional) appears to be on the rise. This is shown by the increased number of families in urban and semi-urban areas that are taking their daughters to doctors to be cut.

Medicalized FGM is an increasing problem in other countries. In Egypt, 78.4% of FGM procedures are currently carried out this way.[10] The primary focus on health issues among early anti-FGM campaigns has been suggested as a contributory factor in families turning to medical staff and facilities, which

9   Katy Newell-Jones, *Empowering Communities to Collectively Abandon FGM/C in Somaliland*, ActionAid, 2018, p. 4.

10   www.28toomany.org/country/egypt.

are perceived to be safer. However, there is evidence that increasing numbers of girls have bled to death on the operating table while having FGM. Additionally, doctors are seen to have more power in society than traditional midwives or cutters, and are therefore less likely to be punished for performing it. A recent study noted that "physicians are not discouraging the practice, giving legitimacy to a procedure that has serious medical risks".[11] Another concern is a lack of knowledge among medical professionals about the functions of female genitalia, or about FGM itself and what it entails. Studies have also shown physicians expressing beliefs that FGM is specified by religious requirements, even defending the practice. Added to this, medical professionals, and especially those in rural areas, have an economic incentive to continue performing FGM.

Even within a specific country, the prevalence varies greatly between regions. For example, prevalence in north-eastern Kenya is 97.5% compared with 0.8% in western parts of the country. This variation helps to explain why eradication has proved challenging, because the reasons the practice continues to persist are vastly different for each community. There is no uniform solution, as a tailored approach is required for each nation and the diverse communities within them. Changing a practice that is deeply entrenched in the culture and social life of individuals only becomes possible when an environment that promotes individual behavioural change has been created. This is best achieved through community-based programmes, which can lead to strong grassroots support for changing social norms.

Achieving cultural change

One common approach to eradicating FGM is to implement laws that criminalize the practice. Within Africa, most countries have

---

11 Stanford University Medical Centre, "'Egyptian women say doctors don't discourage female genital cutting', study finds", *EurekAlert!*, 25 August 2016, quoted at www.28toomany.org/thematic/medicalisation.

some form of national legislation in place to criminalize FGM. While laws on their own will never end it, they are an important statement of intent and demonstrate a commitment to eradicating FGM. Nevertheless, legislation remains a controversial instrument of cultural change, as legal norms can feel imposed and are in conflict with social norms. While there may be arrests or prosecutions, enforcement is often poor if the laws do not reflect popular will, and people are often reluctant to accuse their own family and community members for fear of shame or social repercussions. Legislation can force the practice underground or across borders, or lead to FGM being conducted on girls at a younger age. Attempts to legislate have at times resulted in mass cutting by communities or even by the girls themselves.

In a similar way to criminalization, the approach of treating FGM as a human rights issue can be useful in lobbying states and donors to fund and support FGM programmes. However, such approaches often have limited effectiveness at a local level, as communities see human rights as abstract and externally imposed. This approach often assumes that people will act autonomously and independently to realize their rights. It fails to take into account social norms that place more importance on social relationships and conformity.

The health-risk education approach trains individuals (for example doctors, nurses, midwives, teachers, and facilitators) to deliver messages about the short- and long-term medical implications of FGM to members of practising communities. If undertaken in a non-directive way that builds on people's own experiences, raising awareness about health risks can contribute to changes in views and behaviour. However, some reports have shown that when it does not fit with a woman's personal experience of FGM, she does not respond well to this approach. This is because she may not have experienced these health implications herself, she may not realize that the symptoms she is experiencing are linked to FGM, or she may even deny that she is experiencing health issues altogether.

Eradication requires a cultural shift away from the social norms that encourage the practice of FGM. One of the key social norms to tackle is that of the rite of passage: an action or ceremony in which a child is deemed to have transitioned into adulthood. Within many FGM-practising communities, it is considered a rite of passage for a girl to transition into womanhood. Part of the approach to changing social norms has therefore been to try to find alternative rites of passage (ARP). This is because those who decide not to continue the practice will likely face social sanctions from failing to carry out the rite of passage, such as an uncut girl's inability to find a husband because she is not considered to be a woman.

Embracing an ARP should allow these communities to stop the practice without the usual punishments that come from violating social norms, as new norms have been established. Unfortunately, efforts to find new rites of passage are rarely successful. A survey carried out to assess a 2017 ARP intervention among the Maasai community of Kajiado in Kenya found that while it helped the girls stay in education and also delayed early marriage, it did not make them feel like women in the traditional sense. The ARP was seen as an extension of childhood rather than a fully-fledged transition into adulthood. The reason this method didn't work is that the ARP was imposed externally, rather than being a grassroots, community-led initiative. If the ARP comes from within the community it has a better chance of being seen as a genuine rite of passage. To have an impact, the new social norms must develop organically rather than being imposed artificially, which is where past attempts have fallen short.

Another key issue as to why eradication has proved difficult is the role influencers have within communities, and working out how to shift their opinions on FGM. In some contexts, key influencers within the family are fathers, brothers, and male partners. For example, 88–89% of men and women in Burkina Faso stated that fathers play a critical role in determining whether to have a daughter cut, compared with 38–46% of men and women who said that mothers play a role. In Nigeria, it is the fathers or paternal grandfathers who decide whether or not to request the procedure. There are also instances of older brothers having a say as to whether or not their sisters should be cut, for example in Sudan. Therefore, to eradicate FGM, the views of male family members need to be incorporated into the programmes that are currently in place. Although there are places where male figures do not have as much of a role in the decision-making process, men may also influence the norms supporting FGM by refusing to marry or eat meals prepared by uncut women, or by pressurizing young men to marry cut women and stigmatizing those who don't.

Other important influencers are religious leaders who, although not key decision-makers, can have a very strong influence and authority over the practice. In some contexts, discovering that FGM is not mandated by Islam or Christianity plays a strong part in persuading people to abandon it. Therefore, it is essential to engage with religious leaders when working in communities where there is a strong belief that FGM is performed to fulfil religious requirements.

Another approach to tackling FGM has involved addressing some of the economic factors that contribute to its continuance. It is often an important source of income for the traditional practitioners who carry it out. The response here has been to retrain practitioners to find other ways for them to support themselves, and to spur on change within their communities. The role of a traditional practitioner itself is also valuable to these individuals, as it gives older women prestige and status in their communities. This role as an elder, sometimes known as a "grandmother", is highly valued and gives the woman a lot of decision-making power with regard to FGM and other areas within the female sphere. This means that trying to encourage the elders who practise FGM to find other lines of work is an important part of changing the social norms that contribute to it, as well as making it harder to perform.

As an isolated solution, however, retraining is insufficient. While it may address the economic incentives of performing FGM, it does not address the loss of status and influence for those who decide to abandon the practice. Neither does it reduce the demand for FGM from families within these communities, which means the practice will persist and other community members will simply fulfil the practitioner role instead.

Collective attempts to end FGM

Despite these challenges, there are now many programmes that are collectively attempting to end FGM. One example of a programme that has taken a more holistic approach is the Grandmother Project: Change Through Culture (GMP). This project attempts to promote positive family roles and values within the communities it works with in Senegal. GMP believes that communities are more supportive of programmes – and that programmes are more effective – when more than one of the issues concerning community and development are addressed simultaneously.

Other issues tackled by GMP include limited social cohesion and communication between generations; the grandmothers' culturally designated role to socialize and support adolescent girls; their cultural responsibility for perpetuating FGM; and the notion that grandmothers do not question the practice, even though they understand the risks. One of the strengths of this approach is that it recognizes the role of elders within the community and attempts to bring them into the dialogue, and therefore into the process of eradicating the practice. This facilitates a more organic internal change, rather than one that is seen as externally imposed. The programme increases dialogue between generations and sexes, which also allows for collective action that involves the whole community rather than just one group.

Ours is one of many charities working together to end FGM. Established in 2010, 28 Too Many provides research, knowledge, and tools for those seeking to eradicate the practice in the countries where it is practised. The charity's vision is a world in which every girl and woman is safe, healthy, and lives free from FGM. It takes three main approaches: collecting and interpreting data; influencing influencers (top-down approach), and equipping local organizations (bottom-up approach).

Data is presented in several ways; primarily through country profile reports and thematic papers, with additional research products as required. To support our aims, we make this research freely available globally. Using the data we have collated, we engage key influencers, encouraging them to advocate for change (of policy, legislation, and so on) within their spheres of influence. Based on our research, we develop and distribute advocacy materials and training tools that local organizations can use to bring effective change at a community level. Ultimately, change happens when policy and legislation (top-down) align with community action and education (bottom-up). Our approach is to play a catalytic role in both, and to base our interventions on solid research.

This research has been used in many different ways and by many different people. One example of its use was to educate teachers in Uganda. A social worker travelled to rural south-western Uganda to run a safeguarding workshop for teachers. She spent hours working with them, looking in detail at data gathered by 28 Too Many and examining the social, emotional, and physical repercussions of FGM. She trained the group to recognize girls who had been subjected to FGM before they succumbed to potential complications. The final stage of the workshop included an enthusiastic discussion about how teachers could act to eradicate FGM in their communities.

A year on, she returned to the school and was pleased to see that the teachers had implemented improved policies and safety measures at the school as a result of this training. They had held meetings with local leaders, parents, and others within the community to spread messages about the importance of child safety and the need to be vigilant against harmful practices such as FGM. Further training was given to help teachers promote girls' education and to help them stop girls dropping out of school when they reached puberty.

There has also been a large decrease in the percentage of people still practising FGM in Kenya. Breaking down the most recent data by age group shows that the prevalence for women aged forty-five to forty-nine is 40.9%, while for the youngest age group (fifteen to nineteen) this has fallen to 11.4%.[12] Even though a small proportion of women may be cut after the age of fifteen, the data demonstrates a clear trend toward lower prevalence among younger women.

Mali, where our 28 Too Many researcher lives, has one of the highest national rates of FGM, and there has been little change in recent years. Nine out of ten girls are currently believed to be at risk.[13] Our researcher has seen first-hand how the combined powers of tradition and silence add to the challenge of eradicating the practice. "FGM in Mali is rife," she says, "yet it is a very sensitive subject and not talked about."

Changing attitudes can be difficult, as Malians fear exclusion from their communities for breaking with tradition and speaking out against FGM. However, local NGOs are working to change attitudes through education, and by encouraging discussion within families and communities. Many Malians believe the practice should continue, but our representative has seen signs of hope. One of her friends recently made the decision not to carry out FGM on her young daughter. She praises her friend's enthusiasm and strength of character, and hopes that in time this decision will influence other women. "She can only talk about her choice with trusted friends in the safe space provided by her local church, but the fact that she is talking about it, and helping others understand, is so important."

Women like our researcher's friend need people to join with them in creating discussion and breaking the silence. "It is hard for individuals to stand against this harmful practice," she says, "yet, together, groups of people are a powerful force for change."

---

12 Data in the country profile update (December 2016), www.28toomany.org/country/kenya.

13 In 2014, the figure was 88.6%, www.28toomany.org/country/mali.

Future programmes and research

To work toward a future without FGM, future programmes must focus their work on shifting these views and behaviours within communities. Education can help to change the social norms that lead to its continuation. Grassroots activism involving the men and boys of a community is a useful way to change ingrained social norms. Continuing with and increasing law enforcement, and ongoing work with a helpline for families trying to assist their daughters, are extremely important steps that require perseverance.

Efforts also need to be made to stop families taking their children across neighbouring country borders to undergo FGM as a way of trying to get around laws that are already in place. There is much scope for strengthening legislation and law enforcement's role in tackling the practice. Without the required laws in place, it is even harder to disincentivize the practice, and sufficient protections must be introduced. It is also critical to involve religious leaders in the process and to help communities to combat the perception that FGM is a religious obligation. Future research and statistical analysis is another important part of the process, and clarity of terminology is vital. Unless valuable data can be gathered, it will be hard to fully understand which solutions are required and how best to move forward.

Finally, it is important to raise awareness of the problems of medicalized FGM, and how it can normalize and mask the health problems that result from it. To avoid the growth of medicalized FGM, it will be essential to promote knowledge of the dangers, and how it can be just as harmful and life-threatening as FGM carried out by traditional practitioners.

FOUR:
CALLED AND EQUIPPED

Having received first-class honours for my degree in 2011, I was encouraged by my anthropology tutor to write my final-year dissertation up into an academic paper. I did so, and offered it to three journals. I chose the easiest first, but in the end it was accepted by the one with the highest footnote standards and the hardest to get into: the prestigious *Journal of Gender Studies*. It took nine months to get through all the editing, but the process was worth it, and I was very proud when the pink-covered journal landed on my doorstep. It became a key paper and was used by the UK government to justify committing to end FGM. As one of the publication's most downloaded papers, it is permanently on free download.

All my experiences up to this point contributed to a refining of the concept. I had learned a considerable amount from the five-month Tearfund evaluation project I had completed in 2006, assessing the impact of the charity's work over ten years. I had also benefitted from the six months I spent with YWAM in Colorado, USA, which included a three-month outreach project in Myanmar, Thailand, and China. The experience greatly increased my understanding of cross-cultural issues and the sensitivities of trying to support culture change. It involved learning new skills, facing new experiences, and considering what could go wrong. This helped me build the confidence I needed to face the many challenges that were to follow when I was on my own.

When I volunteered on a two-week Samaritan's Purse teaching summer camp in Belarus for children affected by the Chernobyl disaster, I learned a lot about team dynamics; the key to good projects. I discovered what upsets volunteers and how a "them and us" culture can exist if local country reps and internationals do not work well together. It also taught me how to process some of the trauma I was experiencing vicariously through poor orphanage models, child survivors of environmental cancer, starvation due to parental addiction, and more.

Another project I chose to work on before finally starting my own was with Habitat for Humanity in Sri Lanka. I worked on a house-building project, building from the concrete slab upwards. I learned to plaster, put in windows, mix concrete, and again work as part of a team. We also saw the impact of the 2004 tsunami on tourism, infrastructure, environment, and people.

I had fundraised from friends, family, and church members to take part in some of these projects, which usually cost around £2,000. For Sri Lanka, I made a flip-chart model of a house with windows, a door, a roof and 1,800 bricks. Each brick represented a £10 donation. I collected signatures for each brick of the house and gave everyone a brick receipt. Once completed – thankfully more quickly than I anticipated, thanks to one donor who bought the whole west wing and another who bought the foundation – I was able to laminate the sheet and take it with me. Then I took a photo of the family of four whose house we built, the sheet of signatures, and myself.

I subsequently posted each donor a thank-you card, handmade in Sri Lanka, with the photo of their donation highlighted on the photo inside. This seemed a successful way to build donor engagement and friendship support for lifelong mission. Those cards remained on some people's mantelpieces for years.

Vital provision

After graduating from ANCC, I completed a Certificate in English Language Teaching to Adults (CELTA) course. I wanted to work against FGM in the wider sphere of violence against women, reproductive health, child marriage, and the voicelessness of young girls. My views were influenced by the volunteer roles I had undertaken in north-east Kenya, where there was a great deal of gender-based violence. I spent some time reflecting on my experiences and also talked to other charities, such as International Justice Ministries, Tearfund, Restored, Stop the Traffik, Club Foot International, and others. I wanted to share my potential ideas for ending FGM with them, and to see how they pursued their causes. Meeting the various CEOs helped me assess the stages of development they were at, and how successful they had been.

At the end of my two-year internship with Forward, I needed to work out how to run with my vision. My church wanted to be sure of my calling, and to ensure that I had the appropriate support and the covering of an umbrella organization for mentoring, support, advice, shared resources, companionship, and safety. I had initially hoped this umbrella organization might be Forward, where I had served a two-year internship. We had a couple of meetings to discuss the contract, expectations, terms, and conditions, but in the end the discussions never progressed and my internship ended.

I was very humbled to be offered a number of choices, and after a comprehensive selection process, which required me to attend several three- or four-day assessments, I took my final choice of two to my church. My vicar and some mission team members helped me choose Church Mission Society (CMS), the Anglican Church's mission arm. With a large African geographic spread and a pioneering spirit, it seemed to be the right option.

I also contacted a friend who had set up a subsidiary charity under Tearfund called Restored. I was invited to meet her and her co-director and chair for lunch. Subject to a board ratification, they decided then and there to host me and my small team under their charity umbrella. The mandate of Restored was anti-violence against women (VAW), especially in the church. I attended the charity's weekly team meetings in Teddington as well as most board meetings, away days, events such as New Wine, and a church training day in Coventry, at which I became my church's focal point for VAW.

There was a wonderful church service to celebrate this momentous point in my journey: a partnership with CMS and being sent by my church to begin a life of mission. I was presented with a Swahili Bible by my African manager to mark this moment and was then seconded to Restored. Its chair was there to pray for me and for the beginning of this new era. Many dozens of friends and family members from across the country came to join and support me. I had arranged for us all to have cake at the end of the 9.30 a.m. service and at the beginning of the 11.30 a.m. service, as well as a sit-down catered lunch for sixty. As it was such an important step for me, I also attended the 8 a.m. Communion service with vows of commitment as I birthed my new concept. I wanted this public sending out, as I knew my journey would be hard; I just had no idea how hard!

I believed my longing to end FGM was a vision from God, and felt there was enough general interest that it might be accepted in Africa one day. In time, I received training from Restored, an induction with CMS, and licensing from my church.

I spent a probationary year with CMS from September 2010–11, which enabled me to refine strategies to help end FGM. However, I stated that I did not want to run a charity myself. I thought it would involve a great deal of bureaucracy and made it clear that I preferred to deliver front-line solutions.

I also attended multi-agency safeguarding training run by Essex Police covering the roles of Multi-Agency Risk Assessments Conference (MARAC) and Multi-Agency Safeguarding Hubs (MASH) so I could become better resourced to deal with safeguarding incidents. Although these issues were a little peripheral to my core cause, many women and girls facing FGM had also been subjected to violence – something I was familiar with personally.

I then spent some time with CMS in Nairobi, Kenya. There I met the team responsible for Samaritan Strategy, which enables African groups to take responsibility for addressing issues within their communities. I hoped they might include anti-FGM knowledge in their training workshops, and I was able to share at a few churches while I was there.

Inspired Individual

Around the time that Restored agreed to be our host, I was put forward for a scholarship with Tearfund's Inspired Individual scheme. This was aimed at social entrepreneurs who aspired to do something groundbreaking, and who were looking for financial, psychological, and technical input in the form of mentoring, materials, seminars, conferences, and resources. After completing various forms, references, interviews, and meetings, I was delighted to be picked to take up one of Tearfund's African VAW cohort places, which lasted from 2012 to 2015.

The award offered many amazing benefits. It enabled me to meet others in my position, many of whom were based in Africa and the Middle East. I was also able to share my vision and overall dream with peers across many of the countries in which I was hoping to implement our 28 Too Many research projects once completed, and gain their valuable feedback on applicability.

The Inspired induction/orientation involved addressing the Tearfund head office staff of 250 at Tuesday morning staff prayers and being interviewed. Members of the press, media, and communications team were very interested in what I was doing, and were keen and able to open various doors, which, as a fledgling charity, would not have been possible on our own. These included interviews with *Christianity* and *Woman Alive* magazines, and other media interviews with Premier and UCB Radio, BEN Television, and Revelation TV.

My induction seminar was hosted by the scheme director, the Africa manager, and a South American manager at a retreat house in Surrey. There were four of us on the course: a woman from Iraqi Kurdistan, a man from a disputed country in the Former Soviet Union, a man from Zimbabwe who was living in South Africa, and me. We were asked to share our life stories over a period of up to two hours. We had all suffered some form of trauma, abuse, violence, loss, and cross-cultural transition. One story was so traumatic that it took all my strength not to leave the room. I decided the storyteller would have considered it another rejection if I had left, so I stayed. I had a terrible headache, and had to count and say the alphabet backwards to block out the content. I found it hard to look the person in the eye later, as I felt ashamed of what I had heard.

I had never told my whole story from beginning to end without leaving anything out before. Although exposed, and feeling somewhat naked and shamed afterwards, I also felt released, as if I could breathe more easily, and that I had been unconditionally heard.

The remainder of the time was used to explain what was to happen next, and when. I had time to get to know my mentor, Sean, who had interviewed me twice to join the scholarship programme. We also completed various exercises and baseline tools to benchmark where we were at in various areas, such as finances, self-care, governance, and personal relationships. This gave us all a chance to set our priorities for the three-year journey of the scheme.

One of the things I learned, and that had led me to attend the CMS Pioneer Mission Leadership Training course the year before, was that the life of a founder or leader can be lonely, and that there is a high chance of burnout early on. The first few years involve bobbing along at the bottom of the seabed, investing long hours for little financial or programme return. Then it reaches a point at which opportunities come thick and fast, and the hours, funds, work, and exposure all become overwhelming. The growth curve shifts from horizontal to vertical, with hardly any angle at less then ninety degrees. This often leads to physical, mental, spiritual, and emotional burnout, depression, isolation, anxiety, sleeplessness, and withdrawal. Joining the Inspired scheme and the CMS pioneer leadership cohort helped me gain the support of other social entrepreneurs and thrive rather than dive.

I attended two workshops in South Africa: one with the VAW cohort in the first year, and another in the last year of the scheme. I also attended a couple of leadership workshops in Kenya, which covered governance, founder's syndrome, fundraising, and communications. By the end of these I had a strategy and plan of how to go forward with my vision, which was wonderful. Added to this, I had made good friends in Kenya, Tanzania, Iraqi Kurdistan, and Uganda.

I had face-to-face access to Sean in London as well as phone-based contact for coaching and mentoring sessions. He also met and helped guide my team of managers. The VAW cohorts in Africa also built friendships, yet were split into cliques over different years of intakes, races, ages, and genders at times. We were all visionaries, yet judgments were sometimes made about the plans of others. Some were making a large impact in one specific geographical context, others at a national or even international level. I guess jealousies were also present within a mostly female group of survivors of trauma and violence.

Again, we listened to each other's stories, and while there was a person with us to act as a pastor and offer emotional support, it was hard to walk out and say, "I've had enough" or "Your life story is too much for me". Luckily, I had a good support system in the UK – within my church, the wider church, my board, CMS, and with my team of managers, volunteers, and peers – which proved invaluable.

FIVE:
SETTING UP THE CHARITY

My specific calling to end FGM was well and truly inspired by meeting Fatima in 2005, yet my calling to help the disadvantaged and pass on knowledge was born long before that. Serving at the Red Cross from the age of six to eighteen, the Territorial Army from eighteen to twenty-two, studying business from sixteen into my twenties, and training in neurolinguistic processing, counselling, coaching, and psychology all served as crucial experience in helping me morph from corporate life to a faith-based pioneer calling. I finally felt ready to launch my God-given vision.

As the concept vision caster and founder – the person with the calling and passion to address ending FGM through resourcing others – I was on my own. I would lie awake at night thinking about how to make a difference through a lasting contribution in a way that would empower those in Africa. As an educated, white HR consultant from London, I often thought that if I had been head of God's HR department I would not have chosen me! Instead, I would have selected a medically trained African woman – possibly an FGM survivor or a midwife. Yet I felt God had called me, and all I had to do was obey his calling and do my best, and the rest would fall into place.

My corporate and HR consultancy background had given me skills in brainstorming with sticky notes, yet I was used to facilitating via drawing out ideas from others. As an extrovert, I felt I had no one to collaborate with on this project. I had gained skills and experience from working overseas with Medair, and in development studies at All Nations Christian College (ANCC), so I understood the need for a succinct high-level strategy and a logframe (a project work plan or Gantt chart) to indicate outcomes and measures of success. The difference here was that I had few options to assess.

A friend in Sussex offered me her home for a few days so I could use her dining room as a project "war room". She was out at work all day, so I headed into the room, slightly nervously, with sticky notes, flip-chart paper, tape, and marker pens. As with many projects, it was easier once I got started. By the end of the first day, I had covered most of the room in ideas, concepts, dreams, and possible activities to help eradicate FGM. These included a focus on each of the twenty-eight countries where FGM happens, recognizing the importance of engaging educators, medical personnel, law enforcers, and community members to help end the practice.

Having undertaken my ANCC placement at the IDP camp in Dadaab, Kenya, I had seen the success of engaging circumcisers, religious leaders, elders, parents, men, and youth and their uncut girls and women. Our strategy would need to take into account the differing agendas of all these groups. I had also studied psychodynamic gender-based violence counselling, learning from the tutors and twenty other students about how violence can be associated with poverty, poor housing, and lower levels of education and literacy, and about patterns of violence.

The initial strategy was recorded on sheets of flip-chart paper covered in yellow sticky notes, which were clustered by concept, rolled up, taken home, and typed up. I distilled the information into a high-level vision, mission, and focus. I wanted to work with a top-down approach, influencing the UN, country-level governments, faith leaders, and international non-governmental organizations, including Plan International,

Save the Children, World Vision, CARE, and the Red Cross/ Crescent.

Having visualized the initial calling, it needed to be tested with others who ran similar projects, and with potential beneficiaries in Africa. I arranged to visit two charities in the UK. The first was Viva, which runs ethical children's care projects across Africa. I arranged to spend a day at Viva's head office and met the CEO, COO, operations manager, and other team members. They were extremely helpful and actually said I was ahead of where they had been when they started. I took away a number of documents to use as templates for the strategy and work plan. I was also introduced to a woman who worked for the organization in Uganda so I could meet up with her when I was in Africa.

Then I spent a day at Stop the Traffik's head office, seeing the initial vision, how the charity had staffed up as it grew, what its set-up values had been, and how it had found trustees.

I also learned of mistakes the two charities had made in terms of growth, scale, duplicating the work of others, and establishing a place in the third sector. I left with some questions answered regarding legislation and protocols for a charity, set-up costs, and barriers to overcome before the launch. Given that many charities fail in the early stages, I wanted to learn about applicability, replicability, and scalability for others to expand the work as far and wide as possible.

My plan was to ensure that I was equipped with the appropriate skills, so I arranged a two-week trip to Kenya, which would include CMS's Africa Conference and a week with another non-governmental organization – Pioneers – to attend its East Africa Conference. Here I was able to share and refine my ideas.

It was important for me to gauge whether there was even a need for my concept, which was to produce research reports on each of the countries in Africa that practised FGM at home and in the diasporic populations that had settled elsewhere but often still practised it. These reports would be used by national governments, UN bodies, international and local NGOs, faith-based organizations, media, and advocacy representatives. They could be used by local NGOs to train their beneficiary populations and help educate young people and influencers. I hoped this top-down and bottom-up strategy would act like pincers and squeeze the problem from both ends.

I had calculated that it would take six generations (three initially, plus an extra three for the hard-to-change countries) – requiring every generation to stop inflicting FGM on the next generation. This meant that a girl would not be cut; and she, at the age of twelve, would become a mother and not cut her child; and, at the age of twenty-four, on becoming a grandmother, she would not cut her grandchildren. I thought a realistic success measure would be a 10% reduction in FGM in ten countries over ten years (my 10:10:10 vision). I felt I had formed a reasonable strategy and team.

Thirty people at the CMS Africa Conference and twenty-five at the Pioneers Regional Conference all heard my ideas in presentations. Their positive feedback was hugely encouraging. I also met regional representatives of Club Foot Africa and Viva Uganda, and discussed their strategies. These helped me refine my concept. I sent my rough strategy and vision to an ex-Medair board member, an ex-Medair country director – both aid consultants – and two corporate consultants to help critique my document. I was ready to get going.

Between the years 2010 and 2012 – when I was setting up my project and, as a result, the charity – there was limited knowledge out there on the subject of FGM. I went to a church to share an outline of my vision on how to contribute to ending the practice, and was asked by the panel members, "What *is* FGM?" Instead of spelling it out to them, I just held up the book I was reading: *Female Genital Mutilation* by Comfort Momoh. The feedback I received later amused me somewhat, as they said I was too modest to say those words out loud. The truth was, I spent most of my time talking about FGM, silencing dinner parties and becoming the focal point of many family gatherings. I have never been challenged for being too modest about FGM since this occasion!

The charity name was chosen to represent the twenty-eight countries in which FGM still occurs. The husband of my PA from before we started the charity suggested it when we were brainstorming for an identity. I immediately loved it, as it encourages the hearer to ask, "What is 28 Too Many?" We had to be able to give an explanation in the form of an elevator pitch within the first ten seconds of a meeting.

Finding the right people

I had decided to go on a march to mark International Women's Day on 8 March 2010, and had asked a friend's dad to make me a plywood placard. She and I stapled an End FGM poster onto the plywood and covered it in plastic in preparation for a wet march. I set off on the Underground with gloves and hat, heading for the start at Marble Arch. This was my first march – relatively late in life – and I felt excited, if a little nervous. I had reconnected with an old friend from my corporate British Gas days, and she had offered to meet me. She recognized me by my voice, and we were just taking our photo when another woman approached, attracted by the FGM placard. She had just left corporate law two weeks earlier and was keen to be involved in anti-FGM work. I took her card, and within a week I had recruited her as a voluntary research manager.

Meanwhile, my ex-colleague and I had caught up with each other's news by the end of the march, and I bought her lunch to discuss my ideas for the charity. The following week, she too had come to see me, and we had discussed my big idea, dream, and vision for ending FGM, with good information-sharing. A few drinks later, this friend also agreed to join me as a volunteer for six months. She would do the operations set-up and build the infrastructure, while the other new volunteer would conceptualize the research product, and I would share the vision and raise some funding.

Once I had these two managers on board, we started to see progress. They volunteered for the first six months, and then we worked out self-employed contracts for them as part-time roles. I had spent the first year of 2010–11 fundraising for my own support of £25,000 per annum (pro rata at £15,000 for a three-day week, although I was working a six-day week). My funding came from individuals, friends, and link churches connected to CMS, who were happy to have me as their African missions person.

We found, through synchronicity or God's intervention, that the right people were attracted to us. We were pleased to find a young woman who had a heart for Africa and was looking to volunteer with us. She came from a small church in the USA and we brought her over to the UK to meet us, have an induction, and clarify her remit. She volunteered with us for more than two years, helping with research on the ground in Kenya and Uganda. She had a Land Rover and was happy to research the conditions and reasons behind FGM in different contexts, supported and financed by her church in the USA.

Many members of our initial team and board were Christian in belief, yet we did not want the charity to have an overt faith identity, as it clearly reached out to those of Muslim and Jewish faith, those of no faith, and those with African or other traditional beliefs. We have always aimed to have a board, staff, and volunteer team that fully represents faith, gender, age, disability, sexuality, and racial diversity. Numerically, we have a higher proportion of church funders and supporters, yet we have been open to speaking in other faith buildings and especially to groups of Muslim women. We have had Jewish and Muslim board members, and donors from four faith backgrounds.

We soon needed our inaugural board meeting, and I persuaded three people I greatly respected to become founder members of the organization and board members. One was an experienced accountant, who ran a charity and had worked in Afghanistan. Another had been a teacher in Asia for twelve years, and the third was the chair of Restored. We continued to recruit new trustees annually – usually two per year – until we grew to ten, and then more to cover absence and potential future vacancies. We set up with comprehensive governance and human resource practice from day one, and had a good suite of policies in place within the first couple of years.

We set an annual calendar of events to include four board meetings, a team away day, and a board away day. We also planned to have a cycle of days to mark and commemorate special events that related to FGM. The first of the year was Anti-FGM Day on 6th February, followed by International Women's Day on 8th March. We added Day of the African Child on 16th June and Day of the Girl Child on 11th October. We always marked the Sixteen Days of Activism, from International Day of Elimination of Violence Against Women on 25th November to Human Rights Day on 10th December, encompassing World Aids Day on 1st December. These sixteen days often had themes and campaigns, such as #MeToo and #OrangeTheWorld, to coordinate efforts. Since 2018, we have also engaged in the eighteen-day campaign to End Violence Against Women, encompassing anti-trafficking rights proposed by the Philippine government.

One of the sadnesses we all shared was the death of Ghanaian-British anti-FGM pioneer Efua Dorkenoo, who died suddenly of late-stage cancer. It left many of us totally shocked, and we were suddenly without our mentor, friend, and role model. She is still missed, as a giant upon whose shoulders we all stood. Her death also made us realize that we each have a part to play. Each of us is a piece of the jigsaw – without whose individual contributions, the progress to end FGM will be slower or will not happen at all. Unlike many who have decided to work with or fund overseas programmes, I, like Efua, see research as the key to good funding decisions and ending FGM strategically.

Start-up funding

Funding is essential in the life of small, embryonic charities, and fundraising can be a challenge. Just as new graduates often find it tough to obtain work without experience, yet are unable to gain experience without a job, so it is with funding. It is often hard to generate funds for start-ups as the charity is defined more by its ideas, hopes, visions, and aspirations than by what it has actually achieved. It is almost impossible to secure funding for infrastructure setup costs, such as office space, furniture, computers, printers, telecoms, and so on.

We had held our first board meeting in my kitchen, with five of us sitting around the oak dining-room table made by my grandad, and we set up our office in my former dining room. As I had run my psychology practice and previous HR consultancy from my home, I still had four desks and two computers set up and ready to go. With a year of probation at CMS ahead of me, I had time to get things ready for a proper start in 2011, and a full charity launch in 2012.

I had been successful in raising a couple of thousand pounds a year to go to Belarus and Sri Lanka on trips, and I had managed to match-fund the money given by my church and other supporting churches and donors to go on the YWAM Discipleship Training, I realized the amount I would need to start an anti-FGM project would be in a different league of funding.

I have never thought of myself as a fundraiser. However, at the height of my Medair days I had given a talk at a New Wine women's event, talking to more than 800 women about my work in Kenya. As I shared about Medair's work in Afghanistan, I heard a collective gasp from that large group of women. It was strange, as I had forgotten they were there! Many donated then and there – some giving every penny they had on them. A large number also gave in response to a follow-up letter written in my name by the UK director, which was sent to all those who had already contributed.

I forgot about this event until the next time I attended a Medair board meeting, when the UK director greeted me with "Good morning, fundraiser of the year!" On further questioning, he explained that various people who gave £5 on the day had given £50 in response to the letter. Some then gave £500 a year, and one couple had decided to sell their successful business, worth more than a million pounds, and gift the money to Medair. They did this with the full acceptance of their two children, who would not receive any inheritance as a result. This experience taught me that fundraising is all about the story, and the way a story touches the hearts of others. Just as I touched the hearts of these ladies at the conference with a story of poverty in Afghanistan, I now needed to tell an FGM story that would capture people's imaginations.

One of the criteria we needed to meet in order to register as a charity was to raise an initial £5,000. I had been invited back by New Wine to speak at its women's conference again and share about my mission to end FGM. New Wine did not normally allow fundraising collections, yet at the last minute they decided we could collect funds. All I needed were four volunteers and four large red buckets! I came from the back of the stage and sat in the front row without turning around so I could manage my nerves. Once I stood up, the stage lights were so bright I couldn't see what the audience of 900 women looked like. It wasn't until I spoke about Fatima and her fate from FGM that I heard the sound of 900 women catch their breath in a gasp for the second time in my life.

After my friends had collected their donations, I was amazed to find that we had collected £9,000. One woman had even donated her bus fare home. We could finally open a bank account and start our charity. We just needed to open the bank account first in order to bank the cheque!

Contacts and research

Our research manager travelled with her family to visit Liberia and Sierra Leone. She made some extraordinarily important government contacts, whom she met and interviewed. This meant we had some vital research and could write up a comprehensive report about the situations in Kenya and Uganda; countries where I had also worked extensively.

When I went to Kenya, the first country we planned to publish our country report on, I was amazed that the final list comprised of 149 organizations committed to ending FGM. I shut my eyes and visualized a march to the president's palace of 149 banner-carrying NGO representatives, thinking this could be the people power needed to end FGM in Kenya.

I visited Uganda during the same trip. I had spent quite a lot of time in the capital, Kampala, during my aid work days and also in the north, where FGM rates were highest. The war in Somalia had led to more Somalis being displaced, and many had made Kampala their home. As a result, FGM continued to increase in Uganda as people groups moved and carried on the practice, settling as diaspora in Kampala and swelling the overall Uganda prevalence with the local practising population in the north-east, where our researcher worked.

We decided to focus first on East Africa as a cluster, though each country was very different. I worked closely with our database volunteer and wider research team to make a database of all the contacts I had from working in each country. We then added all the government ministries, UN agencies, international and local non-profit organizations, faith bodies, and other organizations that had started undertaking anti-FGM work. We also sent a research questionnaire to all the educational and medical organizations doing some form of anti-FGM work as part of their offering.

I chose to go to Tanzania and Ethiopia for a research visit to supplement my previous experience in East Africa. In Tanzania I had some dresses made for myself and my host from a slab of fabric given to me in northern Nigeria. She ran a home for fifteen or so street girls and loved them all like family. I wore floor-length dresses there and was involved in her ministry of selling mango juice, and I enjoyed getting to know the country.

I landed in Ethiopia on the second Ethiopian Christmas Day, 6th January (Western Epiphany). I was covered in a travel cloak, as I realized this was a much more conservative country than the others. English was less commonly spoken in Ethiopia, and women did not go out after dusk. The realization that 50% of women there had experienced FGM had a profound impact on me. Ethiopia was also a much more centrally controlled country, making it obligatory to register a mobile telephone with the main post office, to have health immunizations (such as smallpox) even though global eradication had been accepted, and to be particularly sensitive regarding any mention of FGM.

The first person I visited with our report for Ethiopia was concerned about how the government might respond if we included historical human rights events. I had a further taste of this issue when I presented at a government meeting that afternoon. I was asked, "How do you have a list of organizations working against FGM in your report when working on that issue is illegal?" I wanted to protect the charity, the integrity of our report, and the organizations we had profiled, and ultimately to ensure that women who had undergone FGM had access to assistance in Ethiopia. Using advanced diplomacy skills, I suggested that these were the results from our research – and that we were there to clarify points like this. We decided to refer to FGM in slightly different terms in some Ethiopian examples so as not to cause offence, while still ensuring that our report achieved its aims. I heard that some leaders of a well-respected international non-governmental organization had been sent to prison for working on this issue publicly. Other NGOs had been forced to change their name, mandate, and purpose.

Ongoing funding

As funding is so critical to success, yet also difficult to source, it brings with it moral decisions. The process sometimes requires reference back to charity foundational documents, such as Memorandum and Articles of Association, and to mission, vision, and values statements. Our initial funding was easy to accept as it came from New Wine, whose 900 women conference attendees had generously given the money. It came without any restrictions, enabling us to open a bank account and making us feel we had really started our journey.

As these were the early years of FGM being discussed, we were among the early campaigners advocating for its end across Africa, the diaspora, and the world. One day, I received an email from a successful businessman who worked in the retail sector. He wanted to produce a line of underwear and adult pleasure toys branded with our logo, name, and a message about ending FGM. He was very keen to partner with us so we could take a percentage of his sales. The businessman was very persuasive, explaining how he saw it as the perfect sponsorship partnering, as both we and he were committed to enhancing women's pleasure: him through selling sex aids and erotica, and us through fighting for the rights of girls who had needlessly had their genitals altered for non-medical reasons.

I was concerned about what our board, church, and CMS would think of our funds coming from this source! I said I would bring the opportunity to the board, yet felt it unlikely that the proposal would be accepted. I was right. Nearly ten years later, a very successful retailer of sexy underwear and erotic toys partnered with another anti-FGM activist, who modelled some of its clothing and lingerie. Different time, different values, different partnership… same cause.

A few years later we were contacted by an Iraq-based Christian who worked for a major international company. The business spanned many sectors, including one controversial arm. She and a group of women were in a Christian prayer group and wanted to donate a four-figure sum to our charity to help women and girls who had suffered FGM. Again, we considered whether this was a conflict with our values and decided that, as it was a personal donation, we would gratefully receive the gift.

Our most generous and consistent donor emailed us out of the blue shortly after we had formed as a charity. He was a successful businessman and thought his partner might be interested in anti-FGM work, so he had emailed half a dozen charities in the sector, all known to us. To my surprise, no other charity had replied. He was interested in how we ran the charity, our policies, the impact we were making, and our hopes and dreams. After a few emails, we met up at his family home, where I had a fairly thorough interview and met his partner and daughter.

What followed was a generous five-figure donation. Like our other donors, he gave all his donations anonymously and without restrictions – the most flexible way to give for a charity, yet a method that requires trust. We often invited him to events, AGMs, launches, and FGM-related activities. This particular donor is a busy international businessperson, so he was often in a different time zone. Over the years, he has given even larger donations, and in the last few years he has helped with donations-in-kind of a boardroom venue, executive coaching, support, and wisdom. His latest donation was a very large one – seven times the original gift – and it marked his own retirement legacy from a key investment business. He has offered to keep funding us via his other activities for the next few years and is pleased to see his investment in our charity showing dividends, as the impact in terms of the reduction in FGM over the last seven years is clear.

Our final major fundraising initiative involved a very aristocratic lady from Knightsbridge who had connections to the royal family, and who agreed to host a dinner for us. I met her for a discussion at The Ritz. She was immaculately dressed in a cream woollen coat, dress, and floor-length wrap. She sipped sparkling water while I enjoyed a pot of tea and ate her biscuits. Afterwards, she escaped the rain by sailing off in a taxi while I walked to the Underground under my umbrella.

I was unable to make the dinner date as it was double-booked with my trip to West Africa. On top of that, I was unwell with undiagnosed cancer at our pre-event meeting, which she seemed to interpret as a lack of commitment on my part. I had been trying to cover up my general anxiety about my health, yet, as she challenged me, I ended up in tears and explained that I was awaiting test results. I later heard that our survivor speaker arranged for that evening had been very delayed, another survivor had not shown up, and the host had suffered a major panic attack! Thankfully, one of our other survivor friends had arrived just in time, and our operations manager had taken my speaking role. Yet it was a stressful evening all round, and the income generated was fairly insignificant given the work, effort, and investment it had involved, so we decided not to do any more dinners.

Our latest donor is an overseas foundation, and all liaison takes place via a third party for anonymity reasons. Only I know the identity of the donor, and confidentiality is highly valued by all parties. This donor has given four times, and has, like the others, seen how the investment makes a major impact on our niche NGO.

Our only government grant came from the Department of Community and Local Government (DCLG). We were pleased to bid for a community faith grant that would help us work with faith leaders to make a statement about ending FGM. The DCLG opportunity was about funding small, local, community-based projects. We produced 500 packs for faith leaders and delivered training courses across the country, following our role in collecting signatures from faith leaders, which was used at an FGM Summit hosted by David Cameron and others. Our work was held in high esteem by the deputy prime minister in the conference closing remarks. Like all grants, it required a fair degree of administration, paperwork, monitoring, and liaison. We had to make a video of our work and hosted a monitoring and feedback meeting at our accountants' offices toward the end of the project.

We also pitched for two major Department for International Development (DFID) FGM grants – a share of the £35 million and £50 million it was awarding to the FGM sector. We were part of three consortia bidding for different streams, but these were quite challenging processes for a small charity. We were the research lead or expert in all cases, and were pitching for the communications and research bids. Our key partner on the comms bid withdrew very late, owing to the Syrian crisis. So we regrouped, but the team was not as strong as it could have been, and while we had some good feedback we did not have the African infrastructure or established network presence of the winning team.

The research bid was won by a large US research organization. Again, we hoped to work more closely with these individual consortia organizations, yet after the announcements there was less liaison than we had hoped. Additionally, key players moved on to overseas or UK government postings, and some left the sector for personal reasons. The sector is ever-changing, with new survivors joining, and corporate or aid agencies moving on to other causes. These days we tend to adopt an expert advisor role.

I have learned a great deal about fundraising, to the point where I was asked to speak at the Institute of Fundraising's annual conference in 2019. More and more, I see funding as being about legacy and a lifelong relationship. It must be a cause that is close to donors' hearts, enabling them to help a charity and form a relationship – thus becoming increasingly moved by the cause and eventually partnering with it. Win, win.

Partnerships

We have had good relationships with a number of government departments, including the Home Office (HO), Department for International Development (DFID) and the Foreign & Commonwealth Office (FCO). We have had the privilege of sitting on the FGM Forum, which is designed to represent other government departments, along with NGO and activist representatives. Some of the meetings have been quite challenging in terms of the passion of survivors juxtaposed with policy and budgeting constraints, yet we attend diligently and contribute enthusiastically.

We also worked with the Department of Health and NHS England on various issues, including NICE guidelines. I personally helped to ensure that GPs could have a code to use for FGM and for the common implications of the practice, such as urinary tract infections, fistula, sexual problems, and complex birth issues.

One of the highlights of working in this sector is the depth of relationships that have been formed. There are far too many to mention here, yet the founders of Daughters of Eve –

three specialist midwives from the Whittington and Guy's & St Thomas' hospitals, and the lead midwife and policy lead from the Royal College of Midwives – are ones I have respected and enjoyed working with over these last two decades, and I count them as friends. I have also very much enjoyed working with a midwife and sexual health nurse at the former West Acton clinic, and various others with roles in Walthamstow. My duties have involved shadowing their clinic roles, talking on co-speaker panels, being colleagues on steering groups, co-advising at policy development briefings, co-leading workshops, and giving keynote addresses at conferences and media events.

Some of these survivors, ambassadors, and champions have gone on to lead organizations such as the Manor Gardens FGM Forum in North London and Vavengers (an anti-FGM collective), which donated funds for us to turn UK research into an FGM pack and then produce a resource for secondary schools. This followed on from a start made by one of our volunteers, who tragically died of cancer. I attended her funeral in the Lake District, and was touched that her daughter volunteered for our charity after her PhD. We were honoured to be the beneficiary charity of the funeral donations, which will make her contribution – to a secondary-school resource on FGM – all the more poignant. The fact that she and her husband trialled the pack before her death will never be forgotten. In my toughest days, I remember this and keep going, one step at a time, to make my mark on the legacy map.

Sharing our findings

One of my initial dreams was for a website and information portal where all our information on FGM could be shared. This would include the cluster of topics to which FGM related, such as child marriage, fistula, girl child rights, and so on. In the early days we bought a web design and were happy with it for three years. We created weekly blogs, shared our news and research in *The Huffington Post*, and featured across the

Christian media spectrum from the *Church Times* to *Inspire* magazine. We were also very humbled to win a number of awards right from the beginning. As time went on, we translated our reports from English into the key languages of French and Arabic. We also sought translator support from UN volunteers under our translation manager for translations into French, Arabic, Swahili, Amharic, and other languages in order to enable community-based NGOs to access the reports in their first language.

A project that could have been seen as "scope creep" was the fulfilment of thematic reports giving a wide exploration of a particular issue across all twenty-eight countries. These were comparable with the depth of the country reports, which gave information on all the issues in each country. We commenced with medicalization, which highlighted FGM in medical settings. Rates were especially high in Egypt, Nigeria, and Kenya. Two girls had died on the surgeon's operating table in Egypt during the procedure.

What followed was a two-year project on the law and FGM, for which we engaged more than 120 lawyers in thirty countries to complete a comprehensive analysis of the law on FGM in each country. We researched countries that had changed (such as Sudan and South Sudan; Somalia and Somaliland); we included countries for which we had research data, such as the USA and UK diaspora; and we produced reports on social norms in 2019 and model law in 2020. We aim to complete "Faith and the Remainder of the Diaspora" in 2021, and to report on overall findings, statistics, and trends in 2022.

The team

Team numbers have broadly stayed the same over the ten-year journey of 28 Too Many so far, although, as with many organizations, the faces have changed and the roles performed have increased in breadth, depth, reach, span of jurisdiction, and replicability of initiative. We have come a long way from a beginning of three founder trustees and myself as the founder/ executive director, supported by a PA and volunteer operations and research managers. Initially, all members of our team were volunteers, including ten researchers, finance, board secretary, field researcher, and bloggers. We have gradually recruited a hub of paid professional team members who work on contracts for a variety of research projects and can be based anywhere in the world (currently Europe, Africa, and Australia). The roles have expanded and now include the additional need for a statistician, research editor, communications manager, research project manager, board secretary, and translations manager. As we continue to identify new needs, we will recruit accordingly.

The role of founder is always an interesting one. It is usually this individual's dream, calling, and heart's desire that provides the impetus to set up the charity, and the founder usually has the passion to speak to others about giving their time or resources. This means the founder/executive director's role principally involves leading the external aspects of securing funding, attending key conferences, and speaking at events; providing overseas or strategic committee representation and offering key media, TV, and radio interviews; implementing key staffing and board appointments and training; and shaping the strategy and leadership of the organization.

As a founder, I think it's always good to state at the beginning how long you want to stay. I made it clear that mine was a 2010–22 commitment, supported as a missions project in partnership with various churches up to that point. As that time draws nearer, it becomes more important to have a stable team so that any transition is as smooth as possible.

We have collected hundreds of business card contacts over the last fifteen years and used them to form a contacts database. Our photo library is testimony to the thousands of individual stories we have heard from FGM survivors, which I have had the privilege of hearing in person. As I consider a transition to more of a founder–ambassador role, allowing the day-to-day operations to be managed by others, there will be time to tell this and other stories; to encourage young people to get in touch with their own callings, heart's desires, dreams, and visions – and to answer the question: "What legacy do you wish to leave on this earth after you have gone?"

A voice for the voiceless

Our initial vision was to be a voice for the voiceless, and this has truly become our mission. Yet we have seen a shift here. The survivor movement in the UK and overseas has grown in voice and strength, and has become a key player in the field. Providers have come and gone, characters have risen and fallen in status and power, leaders in this sector have changed, heads of state and first ladies have been deposed, and new alliances have grown up and declined. The same demise will inevitably face the current players.

We have gained a good reputation for providing reliable, trustworthy, and accurate information, which can be used by the police, UK and overseas governments, UN bodies, educators, social services, law centres, educators, medics, international and local NGOs, and other organizations. We would still like to see a day when there is no need for our charity because FGM has been eradicated. There is more to do, yet I hope that over the next ten years we will see a marked reduction in FGM, even if it is growing numerically owing to population growth.

Working in a Kenyan orphanage in 2003 for abandoned babies often conceived through rape.

Teaching capacity-building to communities affected by decades of civil war in Southern Sudan in 2004.

Training county leaders in Northern Sudan in 2005 on how to become sustainable project managers.

Make Poverty History: Talking to my MP, Teresa Villiers, about FGM as part of Tearfund's "Tea Time for Change" campaign.

Talking to Anne Coles about my sense of calling at New Wine, which resulted in £9,000 worth of donations from 900 women in 2009.

Studying midwifery in northern Pakistan in 2010.

The first baby I ever delivered as a midwife.

A thank you ceremony held at the end of my time working on the fistula project in Northern Nigeria.

My commissioning to mission service at St Barnabas with vicar Henry, CMS team members, and All Nations College staff in 2010.

Preaching at an indigenous Maasai church that started after two local girls learned that FGM was not a good idea on health grounds and ran away. One became a teacher and the other a social worker.

Engaging with Maasai children on the subject of British and Maasai hairstyles, 2011.

Talking to female Anglican church officers about FGM in Kenya, where the prevalence was around 25%.

My first 10K in London for 28 Too Many, along with my housemate Angela.

My first appearance at the United Nations in New York in 2012, where I managed to get FGM into the statutes.

An annual women's rights campaign event at the Royal Festival Hall in London to launch a new Home Office stance against FGM with other advocates from the sector.

Talking to the police commissioner (centre left) about efforts to eradicate domestic violence and FGM.

Speaking at the CMS stand as a pioneer to end FGM at Greenbelt on its fortieth anniversary.

Receiving training as part of a Tearfund scholarship for social entrepreneurs in East Africa, 2014.

Talking to teachers and students at a school in the Gambia about the dangers of FGM.

Appearing on Premier's *Woman 2 Woman* show with Maria Rodrigues.

Receiving one of the first British Citizen Awards for my work to end FGM globally.

Receiving the global Advertiser of the Year Clio Award, donated by Ogilvy & Mather, for our "It happens here" campaign.

A 28-mile wheelchair marathon, which raised around £18,000 for the charity to finish our research on each country in 2018.

Becoming a pioneer lay minister in the Church of England in 2017 with Bishop of Edmonton Rob Wickham (above) and with FGM advocates Joy and Comfort (below).

Department for International Development (DFID) representatives were visitors at 28 Too Many's 2015-16 AGM.

Attending the Civil Society Forum in Geneva with my PA Selina to mark the twenty-fifth anniversary of the Beijing Declaration and to ensure that FGM remained on the global agenda.

Making a documentary about the work of 28 Too Many with Revelation TV in 2019.

Attending the launch of the NHS National FGM Support Clinics with Selina in 2019.

SIX:
OPPOSITION, SETBACKS, AND ENCOURAGEMENTS

Whenever people ask me, "What do you do?" and I say, "I run an anti-FGM charity", most assume the work is rewarding and well received. They do not expect to hear that it is often met with overt or covert opposition, frequently from the least-expected places.

I guess I should not have been surprised by a number of setbacks when I retrained to pursue my vision of forming an anti-FGM charity. Having been involved in aid work from 2001 to 2005, and with various NGOs across Africa, the USA, Europe, the former Soviet Union, and South East Asia from 2005 to 2010, the challenges should not have come as a shock. Yet, in reality, the surprise related to where the threats came from, not to the fact that they existed.

When I worked at Medair, opposition often came in the form of spiritual attack or spiritual opposition. On one occasion in northern Uganda we were commissioning a new compound, and the local witch doctor and dancers were invited to do a cultural dance around the clinic and sleeping quarters as a form of blessing. The dancers had adapted to a more modern modesty of wearing bras with their cultural skirts, but to me this looked quite odd – effectively dancing in underwear in front of a mostly young, male, Christian team. I was not sure this was a good idea.

Spiritual warfare is a strange one to explain, and it is sometimes reasonable to draw lines. The Medair leaders did not wish to cause offence and the locals wanted to bless the NGO in their spiritual, ritualistic way. Did they invoke any witchcraft spells? Did any of the disharmony, accidents, or problems that followed for the team have anything to do with the spiritual dance ceremony? Even if curses were put there, did they have any power? Should we not believe that our God was bigger than that and could stop all other evil?

In the early years, I experienced considerable opposition from leaders who seemed to be blocking me from getting going. While at All Nations Christian College in 2007–09, I was keen to do an overseas placement in my middle summer. I applied for a post in Nigeria with a Christian NGO that had, in the past, been part of CMS, but had broken away as it felt CMS was becoming too liberal. It seems my application for a three-month placement as a counsellor/tutor was rejected as I had been divorced in 1994. What made me sad was that I had had no choice in the divorce, as my husband left after my parents died. Had I stayed in that marriage I am not sure I would be here today, and I certainly wouldn't have achieved what has come to pass.

I challenged the placement decision and was told I could face a divorce assessment panel – which I was happy to do, though I explained that I felt this was somewhat over the top for a three-month summer placement, when I imagined no one would know whether or not I had been married or divorced. I had remained unmarried since the divorce, so I couldn't see any huge issue. In the end, the placement seemed to disappear – though I said I would be happy to help the organization review its HR policies in this area to ensure they were fair to all parties. Unsurprisingly, this offer was never taken up! Church bodies can unwittingly cause hurts to deepen in situations like this, making them less appealing to others outside the church.

Instead of Nigeria, I secured a placement at the IDP camp on the Kenyan–Somalia border.

A previous time I had gone to work overseas, opposition came from my church vicar, who had been reading the news that morning on the atrocities of the war in West Darfur. I think he was worried I would end up coming home in a body bag. But unlike almost all of the twenty other mission workers from my church, I knew I was called to work in areas of disaster and trauma with issues of FGM and violence against women. I always do a comprehensive risk assessment and serve under an NGO, so I aim to reduce my risks. I have also had kidnapping, evacuation, and other war zone re-enactment training. That said, it has not always protected me from risking more than my fair share of nine lives!

One of the main challenges of starting 28 Too Many, and one that has continued and become more complex, is that it is a matrix organization made up of a dispersed team based in many countries. The focus in the first three years (2010–12) was on establishing the concept of research, carrying out a needs assessment, an options evaluation, resource sourcing, and timeline planning of goals. In the early years, most of us were based in the UK, with a researcher in the field in Kenya or Uganda. We are now based in four UK cities as well as in Germany, Switzerland, Australia, Mali, Uganda, and Kenya, with a research team in multiple locations. We also have a board of up to ten trustees based in different cities. One of the solutions to this challenge was for the management team working in London, Germany, Switzerland, and Sussex to meet quarterly.

If you were to plot the pace of change as a curve on a graph, it escalated at a much steeper angle in 2012. I was aware from my previous studies of the tipping point of change – particularly dangerous for pioneers and entrepreneurs, who are prone to burn out as an idea takes off, leading to a vertical increase on the curve. This could be measured in pressure of commitments; requests for work and speaker engagements; resource demand and funding needed; and the need for policies, risk assessment instruments, and governance requirements, to name just a few of the challenges.

One of the issues associated with running an organization is deciding what to do in tough scenarios. One such day, an account director from Ogilvy & Mather telephoned me out of the blue. She explained that a fee-paying client had commissioned an advertising campaign entitled "FGM: It happens here" for poster sites and bus panels. After a short conversation and listening to her proposal, I summarized by asking, "Are you saying that we can have this campaign in our name for free?" She confirmed this was the case, and I said that I would get back to her. From my position, it seemed to offer an amazing opportunity, and I could imagine little resistance internally, let alone externally. I was wrong there! Interestingly, my communications manager was concerned that it would upset FGM survivors. While I had considered this, I felt a greater good would be served by getting the message out to a wider audience.

One of our board members was an FGM survivor. I asked my colleague to speak to her, then spoke to her myself. After that, I spoke to the chair and received the backing of the board. This sort of thing takes time – usually evenings and weekends as well as long work days. I finally got the sign-off from my chair, and although my FGM survivor board member felt uncomfortable with the campaign she agreed to support it. My communications manager was less happy. In the end, I decided that an opportunity like this rarely comes around for a small charity, and that it was my job to seize the opportunity. We did not have long to decide, so once I had committed we had work to do on copy, design, messaging, and the launch. The launch went well, and it was amazing and surreal to see our logo on anti-FGM banners and buses across London. I never imagined it would have such an impact so soon.

I was travelling with work in Africa when the campaign launched, and was surprised to see another FGM survivor, involved with a different charity, speak out about how much she disliked the campaign. The newspaper printed, "Dr Wilson was unavailable for comment", even though I was never contacted!

When I saw this survivor later, she was just as friendly and chatty as always, and it seemed that all was well between us. People say there's no such thing as bad publicity, but in this case I'm not so sure.

Shortly after this, another anti-FGM charity accused us of disrespecting them with its partner NGO in Tanzania. This was untrue, yet, once again I received a very formal and threatening letter from its board chair. I contacted our chair and insurance company, and sought legal advice on how to respond. I told the lawyer what had happened, and his first response was, "Is that it?" That made me feel much better! We discussed cases of slander and how to sue and countersue, which all seemed very unnecessary. As usual, I wrote and calmed it all down, formally denying any disrespectful action on my part while in Tanzania.

The UK CEO and I met a while later at a European FGM event in Coventry. She referred to the incident, so I suggested we went outside and discussed it there. I somehow felt the Holy Spirit's presence and ended up saying, "I swear on the death of both my parents that I never said or did anything I was accused of." I also said, "As it is not me, it can only be you or the Tanzanian partner, and only you know which it is. Either it's them or it has to be you!"

The conference recommenced, and I have never heard anything on the matter since. Yet again, it was a waste of energy, time, and resources – and, perhaps as some would believe, a case of spiritual attack. I feel safer when I have a lot of intercessors keeping me covered in prayer to avoid getting involved in distracting issues like these.

Early encouragements

There were many reasons for me to celebrate during the first few years, for example learning basic midwifery, and running a fistula rehabilitation project in northern Nigeria. Most of the progress made during the first two years was in preparation, investment, and planning. We went from me harbouring a dream to having a team of three professional managers supported by a complement of volunteers, a board, and a healthy bank account of donations for a start-up. Instead of feeling as though I was alone, I had a group of people supporting my pioneering vision.

Some of this was acknowledged externally when *Inspire* magazine chose to put me on the front cover of its September 2011 issue. A surprising number of people from across the UK, and even a former ANCC student from Sudan, saw the corresponding article. The Sudanese student saw it while home on leave, as many churches subscribed to this magazine for their parishioners. It also seemed that readers voted on their favourite featured people, and I was surprised on opening the post one day to have been invited to an awards ceremony at the House of Commons, which included a cream tea. I went with Jill, who was one of our board members, chair of Restored, and the admissions secretary of ANCC. She also happened to be the one who had recommended me for the article. I was amazed and delighted to be picked as the runner-up in the Inspiring Individual category. It was so encouraging. We had only just started our organization, and the award gave me a sense that I had been right to follow this path, that God was watching, and that the church was ready to receive this work.

By 2012–13, we had grown into a fully-fledged charity with five staff members, a board of trustees, and more than twenty volunteers across several countries. Those years saw us publish our first full-country report on FGM in Kenya,[14] and we also produced two research papers: one for Tearfund and the other for the *Journal of Gender Studies*. We joined professional networks, such as the Gender and Development Network, and gave presentations at more than fifty events, including the UN Commission on the Status of Women and various conferences around the world.

In addition to this, our activities were cited by the UK Department for International Development. Serious fundraising

14 www.28toomany.org/country/kenya.

also began to move forward, seeing us raise some £55,000 in a year for the first time. Over the course of the next two years, our annual income grew to £102,000.

The following two years saw considerable expansion of our activities, with the team producing and completing detailed reports on FGM for nine African countries along with four further country reports. We launched a new project in Kenya, working with local schools to deliver anti-FGM messages to more than 1,750 children and their teachers. In the UK, we worked with the Department for Communities and Local Government to develop new training on FGM for faith leaders in the UK and across Africa, training them to lead change in their communities. In all, we delivered talks or training to more than 5,000 people in the UK, Europe, and Africa, enabling FGM awareness to be widely spotlighted.

The most positive news in early 2015 was being awarded a British Citizenship Award. I was nominated by a friend who has known me all my life, and who did some branding consultancy for us. She was delighted to hear that I had been selected, and we attended the ceremony at the Palace of Westminster, which included an afternoon tea. There followed various photo opportunities and champagne at Church House, and a couple of members of the team came along to support me and my nominator. There were a number of other winners, but mine was the only award for overseas work. I gave a small speech and received my ribboned award from Baroness Cox and Linda Robson (of *Birds of a Feather* fame!).

A major setback

Nevertheless, 2015 was a tough year. It was my last year of being an Inspired Individual with Tearfund, and as I flew to my graduation in Kenya in mid-May I had health concerns on my mind. I was flying with Sean, my mentor, and, as I checked in at the airport I called a very close friend to tell her about my worries. I had found a small lump in my groin/hip socket only a week before, while I was in Uganda addressing Pastor Medad Birungi's conference of 4,000 people. It was only a few millimetres across, and I thought it was a lymph node, enlarged because of tiredness and stress, or simply showing due to heat-related weight loss. When I returned from that excellent trip, it seemed bigger – or actually completely different; more of a lozenge shape, like a hernia.

I was grieving the loss of the man I loved dearly, who had been in hospital for nine months awaiting a heart transplant. I had decided that, on my next visit, I would suggest marrying in hospital and working out the life logistics later. My charity work had become more stable by this point, so I could have worked from any UK location. I never could have predicted that he would be offered a heart in the middle of the night, resulting in a tissue rejection from which he never recovered.

The impact of his death was huge, resulting in weight loss, and making me very tired and sad. I also suffered with night sweats and, although I didn't credit it with any importance at the time, I had a patch of skin on my calf that was extremely itchy. A doctor's visit had put the symptoms of weight loss, fatigue, and night sweats down to grief and the perimenopause. The other symptoms – the lump and itchy patch – were not mentioned. I later learned that my symptoms were a manifestation of the five key markers of lymphoma.

I initially visited my GP for an update on some pains in my hands, which had been X-rayed previously, and the GP advised that it was age-related wear and tear – a term I hate! She wrote one referral for my hands and another for my arms. It seemed crazy that they couldn't be seen together!

I told her there was something else I needed to discuss, and she said, "You're only supposed to only address one issue." I said it would be quick, to which she replied, "Nothing is ever quick!" I said I had a lump in my groin, so she suggested I get up on the couch. As she looked at it, she immediately said, "This is serious." She got out her ruler and measured it. I was offered a two-week sick note, though the doctor correctly said, "You probably won't use this."

I ran home, having been told I would received a referral letter in the next two weeks. My PA asked if it was OK when I arrived. I sat down, saying, "I don't know. I don't really think so."

I kept busy, telling a few close friends about my concerns and asking about twenty people to pray. I had no idea it was as serious as it was. I had never heard of lymphoma as a blood cancer; only leukaemia. I googled "lump in groin" and it suggested orthopaedic issues or issues that I didn't have, as I didn't have all of the symptoms. I subsequently found another cluster of lumps under the first, and returned to the doctor three days after the initial appointment. She said this was common, as they were all part of the lymphatic system. I had to wait for the two-week hospital referral, so life went on, although I felt pretty tired. When the referral letter came I saw that it was from the haemato-oncology department, which gave me a pretty good idea as to the nature of their concerns.

I wasn't easily able to focus on work, but I went to meet a close friend and her daughter for breakfast one day, then to Southwark Cathedral to take Communion before meeting my former Inspired mentor Sean for a coffee. In between, I watched an act of *The Tempest* at the Globe Theatre. Anything to distract myself! I shared my health issues with my cousins during our Lake District holiday that Easter, then called the hospital to confirm my haemato-oncology appointment.

I was due to go to Senegal, the Gambia, and Mali with a friend in two weeks' time, so I agreed to have a week of tests while my consultant was on holiday so he could analyze the results before I returned a week later. I had blood tests, then a PET-CT scan, a painful tumour biopsy, a chest X-ray, and a bone biopsy.

It was hot on the way home, and I'd been pumped full of drugs and messed around, so ideally I needed a seat on the tube. My friend asked for one for me, but the woman sitting in the disabled seat said, "I need it." Other passengers were horrified! It made me realize that some issues are invisible, so I rang Transport for London (TfL) the next day to suggest a badge similar to the established Baby on Board badge. They agreed and said the TfL working group would liaise with me. Little did I know that I would help make this badge happen and then launch it on the 6 p.m. news!

I left instructions that unless I needed to fly home immediately I would complete my West Africa trip, then booked a follow-up appointment with my consultant for the beginning of July. There would be six weeks of waiting, three of which would be spent in Africa. In hindsight, it was probably a bit crazy to go when I was possibly quite ill. The old me was still running the show and thought that missing the trip would be hugely wasteful in terms of the airfares, accommodation, and other plans I had made. We arranged for my companion to receive any bad news that would require me to come home immediately via a friend in the UK who had accompanied me to all my appointments and tests. I reckoned that if I was really ill, three weeks would make little difference. And if I wasn't, everything would be fine! Somewhere deep inside me, I was concerned that if I didn't go to Africa at that stage I might never go again. I did not need special insurance, as I had received no diagnosis and was considered fit to travel.

On the plane, I wrote a bucket list of twenty-five items and suggested my companion did the same so we could compare. She assumed I must have seen *The Bucket List* movie, but as I hadn't, and it was on the Virgin entertainment channel, I sat back in my seat and enjoyed an ice cream while I watched it. My own list has grown and shrunk since then – eighty-four activities recorded and nearly fifty completed. I started doing one a month from January 2016, and should have them all completed before I retire, when life is likely to become one long bucket list!

On balance, I'm glad I went on the trip, but the cost was high. My feet were in a dreadful state, with awful swelling, bruising, and discolouration. In hindsight, I imagine my lymphatic system was not working properly, and I probably needed diuretics to reduce the fluid retention. In forty-degree heat, it was a stress on my body, and six flights probably didn't help! I should have been given some health advice – take aspirin, wear compression socks and a face mask, and so on – yet with no diagnosis I carried on as if I were completely well. Maybe it was better that way, as the three weeks of useful activity helped to distract me from thinking about the illness. And the mission workers we stayed with covered me in prayer.

My results arrived the day after I arrived home. They confirmed that it was cancer, and that chemotherapy would begin within three weeks. My consultant was clever with his choice of language: "As we suspected, we're dealing with a lymphoma," he said. I remember wondering whether one could have such a thing as a benign lymphoma. It would seem not. Apart from him sharing that there were thirty-eight types, I don't remember much of what he said, which is quite common, apparently. Because of this, I now have someone accompany me to appointments so they can take notes and remind me to ask any questions I have prepared, as I am likely to forget, even if I take a list!

More blood tests followed, and he explained that I needed to have six initial double doses of chemotherapy (twelve one-day infusions) every three weeks. These would start three weeks later. He told me it could be Hodgkin (HL) or non-Hodgkin lymphoma (NHL) – and it turned out mine was the latter. I asked, "Is that the good one?" He replied, "It's not really like that." It was a tough question, as NHL is incurable. I could only have four cycles of treatment: this first one, then twelve more doses over two years at eight-weekly intervals, followed by two cycles of stem cell transplant from me, then from someone on the donor transplant list.

The cancer staging came later. I was diagnosed with Stage 3b cancer, which was treated as Stage 4 as mine was aggressive. It was quick-growing; present in my spleen and in all four body quadrants. In fact, it was everywhere except my bones. The PET scan was very depressing, as there were many black patches across my body, including my armpits, hairline, neck, groin, stomach, and chest wall. By the time I had chemo, I could feel twelve lumps externally.

I had found a lump in my neck back in 2012, and the consultant in maxillofacial had said that I needed an ultrasound and biopsy. The radiographer was busy, as it was the 23rd of December. He had said, "It looks fine. If you were my wife or daughter, I would say don't have a biopsy, as we don't like to do unnecessary procedures, but it's your choice." Lying on an examination bed in just a hospital gown, with a gowned and masked man leaning over me, I felt uncomfortable, so I declined the biopsy. In January 2013, I was told that it was fine. A year or so later, I mentioned it to my doctor, and she said not to worry about it – though it never went down. My problem now is that I cannot prove that this lump from 2012 has spread to other areas of my body since then, but my friends working in ear, nose and throat (ENT), and endocrinology felt I had received very poor care. I could have been given radiotherapy for Stage 1 cancer in 2012 and received a good prognosis. As it is, I now have late stage, incurable cancer.

I was heading for a Devon mini break the day of my cancer staging, and I texted a few people the results as I travelled to Torquay on the slow West Coast train. At one point, a tear escaped from my eye as I thought to myself, "No one on this train knows I have just received this news."

I enjoyed some escapism in Devon for five days, with a quiet, calm ex-missionary friend who had a retreat flat in her housing complex. We enjoyed some trips out in nature, on the bus, and in the city, and I chilled out over late breakfasts and baths. We also talked over what needed to be done, and who else had to be told. I decided I would keep working, and she agreed to remain a 28 Too Many trustee for as long as was needed.

Life took on a different pattern from that point. A very close friend and her husband drove from Dorset to stay with me overnight before taking me to London for my treatment. We were there until 5 p.m., then had a bag of medication to take home for the next three weeks. I received my first two chemo doses as an inpatient. I had been too unwell to start with, so I stayed in hospital for a week until I had got rid of an infection, which delayed the treatment. I was pleased when the chaplain visited me with Communion and cheer, and I experienced first hand what a valuable role this was.

Overall, I did pretty well through the chemo. I kept my hair, although I had it cut very short as it thinned. The worst symptom, for me, was the nausea – managed by palliative care – and by the end of the treatment in March 2018 I was on about nine anti-emetic tablets. The nausea lasted for two-and-a-half years from the start of the chemotherapy. My bones were fragile and osteoporotic, and I had a lot of chemo fatigue, leading to diminished memory and cognition, as well as forced menopause. All of these issues require adjustment and add to the overall woes of a cancer diagnosis.

I have been blessed with two excellent oncology clinical nurse specialists (CNS), who have walked the journey with meand have become friends and confidants. The couple who came up from Dorset every three to eight weeks over the space of three years have also been amazing rocks from which I have been able to shift my ever-changing sense of "normal".

Another bright spot came when our charity's advertising campaign, "FGM: It happens here", was put forward for a Clio Award (honouring excellence in advertising) in 2015. We were nominated alongside Ogilvy & Mather, the agency that had created and run the campaign. I had just had my fifth chemo session and really wasn't up to the travel to New York to receive the award if we won. I was sad not to attend, but pleased that our survivor trustee could go on our behalf. She was a total hit, receiving a standing ovation and appearing in the top-ten highlights video. She was flown business class, accommodated in a penthouse suite, and wined and dined. It was such an experience for her!

The organizers of the Clio Awards learned of my situation and sent me a second award, so I had a presentation in London in front of thirty or so people. It took place just after a chemo session, and Mandy, my chemo buddy, and some other friends joined me, as well as our vicar and his wife. Also present were a number of key donors, church leaders, and special friends – one of whom flew in from Switzerland for the event. I felt dizzy with overflowing joy and had scrubbed up as well as I could in my post-chemo state. My close friend was staying and borrowed one of my West African dresses. She paid for us to go to the hairdressers so we felt as glam as could be. Ogilvy & Mather put us up in the London penthouse suite overlooking the Thames, and six of us travelled there from Barnet in a taxi.

We had two parallel launches: one for the London team, and one in New York for the actual awards. What special nights they were! I still look at the golden statue and have to pinch myself that we, 28 Too Many, won Global Advertiser of the Year – knocking the likes of Nike, Amazon, and others with multi-million-pound budgets off the top position. We took home about fifteen other category awards. I felt moved, humbled, and so proud of my team.

Nevertheless, the cancer diagnosis had a major impact on my team, and a number of managers left quite quickly. Most of my team had left within five months, though a couple of key staff members stayed. I met with Sean, who had left the Inspired programme and relocated to Germany, at a coffee shop in London. I asked if he was interested in any of my vacancies – especially the operations manager role – and he accepted! I took his CV to the board the next day and recommended appointing him for a year. The two of us tried to restore stability to 28 Too Many, but these changes cost me dearly, as I had counted many of my colleagues as friends. I have learned to be somewhat more resilient and robust since then, and now try to take things less personally. Yet I miss those relationships, and I still think about and pray for those team members.

This was the first real crisis the organization had faced. Maybe we would have faced some key departures anyway when we hit the storming stage of team development – a bit like the toddler tantrum phase for an organization. Additionally, some people had come for the start-up phase but didn't want to, or couldn't, deliver the established phase of 28 Too Many. Four years on, and a number of volunteer, student, and temporary PAs later, I believe we are entering a more stable period. As of 2021, we have a core team of three and another seven alongside us.

Progress

Our international work developed apace, with country reports on FGM in Senegal and Burkina Faso completed. We contributed to the UN caucus meetings in Geneva to ensure that FGM was included in the new Sustainable Development Goals (SDGs). Here in the UK, we contributed chapters and case studies to three books on FGM, provided expert witness statements, and peer-reviewed two academic papers. We also continued our collaboration with the Oxford University branch of Lawyers Without Borders. A grant from the UK's Department for Communities and Local Government enabled us to equip 400 UK faith leaders to become anti-FGM trainers, and I was selected as FGM expert to work on the first HM Inspectorate of Constabulary (HMIC) police service inspection on honour-based violence and FGM.

By 2016, we gratifyingly found ourselves halfway to our initial goal of seeing a 10% reduction of FGM in ten countries in ten years (10:10:10). I spoke at eighteen key events, including international conferences, and we saw increased involvement from media organizations and social media internationally.

In the same year, I was honoured to be invited to become a fellow of the Royal College of Arts for services to the sector. Another accolade came in the form of being selected as a *Good Housekeeping* heroine for my FGM work, alongside a woman in the navy helping to rescue asylum seekers from the Mediterranean, a woman in the army who lost her foot when her Jeep hit an improvised exploded device (IED), and a woman working to prevent Muslim girls in secondary school from being radicalized and becoming Jihadi brides. We had a wonderful three-day weekend makeover, and then featured in *Good Housekeeping*'s Christmas special!

Several international law firms were commissioned via TrustLaw, Thomson Reuters Foundation's global pro bono legal programme. Through them, local counsel was engaged in more than thirty countries to undertake initial research into legislation relating to FGM. More research resulted in further reports and country profiles being published. Our website was substantially updated and enhanced, and the charity's team grew considerably.

The following couple of years to the end of 2018 saw our research efforts focused on our ground-breaking "The Law and FGM" project.[15] Twenty-eight country reports on laws affecting FGM were published, evaluating what was working and where gaps existed, and suggesting future actions. We continued our representation and participation at multiple events, and maintained ongoing engagement with UK government initiatives, working with DFID, the Home Office, and the Metropolitan Police in London. At the same time, we were engaging with grassroots activists in Africa, participating in joint campaigns, and strengthening our support for local activists and NGOs in our key twenty-eight countries. Our website was completely upgraded to become a global reference library for FGM in Africa, and the translation of material into French and Arabic was initiated.

Our latest campaign, the #NoFGM ribbon, won a silver Clio Award in 2019 and has gained global momentum. The aim is to have one identifiable, unifying brand and logo for all anti-FGM organizations globally to ensure instant recognition and then gain the benefits of repeated recognition to move toward engagement. Although awards are only one indicator of success, they are helpful in sharing our work further and more widely than might be possible without this external measure of impact and evaluation. They also help our donors see that we use their funds well to achieve beyond our size and means. Here's to the next campaign!

Our fourteenth country profile – on Somalia and Somaliland – was published in 2019, and, gratifyingly, we saw laws against FGM being drafted in both countries. We also started mapping the prevalence of FGM within African communities in the diaspora.

---

15 www.28toomany.org/static/media/uploads/Law%20Reports/the_law_and_fgm_ v1_(september_2018).pdf.

Overall, the setbacks have been more than balanced by the encouragements. As I reflect back on nearly ten years of charity annual reviews, I am amazed at the huge progress we have made. We have been awarded for our work many times, including the Global Collaboration Award for our collaboration with TrustLaw in 2018. This time, I did get to fly to New York with my PA and research manager. We were also awarded Best Collaborative Award at the Lawyer Awards. Both awards were given for our law reports.

However, none of our successes and achievements came easily. All were hard won as a result of the commitment, dedication, and efforts of our staff and many volunteers internationally. The challenges, obstacles, and frustrations were numerous. Over the years, we have found ourselves driving hard against a tide of cultural norms, beliefs, and imperatives. In affected countries, gender inequality was compounded by silence and taboos. We often found inadequate legislation or enforcement in place in those countries, coupled with justification of FGM by some religious authorities and the complicit involvement of health professionals. All this – along with a lack of education and public awareness about FGM, and high levels of illiteracy among the women affected – presented further barriers. These factors, combined with inevitable political difficulties, have presented considerable challenges as we attempted to progress our work.

SEVEN:
STORIES OF HOPE AND SEEDS OF CHANGE

The convent school I attended from the age of four was run by nuns of the Holy Cross, and we were divided into four houses. We were encouraged to give from our pocket money to missions in Africa: education and feeding programmes, with the addition of spiritual education. I remember using wax crayons to colour the images of a boy and girl, and choosing their baptismal names of Michael and Susanna. Although I cringe now at the cultural insensitivity of the exercise – and the very English names – this emphasis on mission gave me a heart for others. Hearing stories from my vicar, who had served in Sudan, continued to keep that spark alight as I moved on to grammar school and was confirmed.

More than thirty years later, I shared stories at my old secondary school, Beaconsfield High School, which chose 28 Too Many as its international charity of the year, enabling us to be awarded numerous fundraising gifts for two years. I had the privilege of joining an old school friend who was a class teacher there, and teaching in a school assembly, leading a sixth-form forum, and attending and inputting into various lessons and teacher discussions in the staff room. I hoped to empower other girls to reach their goals by showing them that an old alumna could still run a charity after leaving school at sixteen.

Stories

Stories play a key role in what we do. We hear women's stories through the field work we do on the ground in each of the twenty-eight countries, and these stories help to teach or train professionals; inspire donors to give; educate community groups as to what happens elsewhere; and help policymakers see how change can happen.

I have listened to thousands of FGM-related stories, but I don't always see the whole picture. In some cases I know the beginning but not the end; in others, I know the end but not the early years. Given the language issues, frequent movement of people, and lack of telephone signal, technology, and money, this is not surprising. I am often asked what happened to Fatima, the ten-year-old I met in West Darfur. Although I don't know how she and her child fared in later life, I often think of her and the way she shaped the second third of my life more than anyone else.

We either hear the stories directly, by sitting with community groups and asking them to tell us their experiences, or via our close relationships with NGOs – whether they're community- or faith-based; national or international. We also gather and share stories via trusted websites, social media, hosted webinars, media, conferences, policy discussions, and individual survivors. I have personally heard more than 3,000 stories from survivors, including many from the IDP camp in Dadaab, Kenya; at the fistula clinic I helped run in Nigeria; and from UK survivors, many of whom I now count as friends.

The shared purpose of stories is to give hope to survivors that change *can* happen and *is* happening, and that the reality of FGM as a harmful practice will one day end, as foot-binding did in China. Historically, another role of the story is to give a voice to voiceless women. These women have often been silenced by family members and communities where misogyny and patriarchal norms prevail. Sharing their stories gives them a voice.

Hannah and Grace

One story where I know more about the ending, having revisited the community twice and seen the community worker more frequently, is that of Hannah and Grace. These Maasai girls were ten and twelve years old when famine struck Kenya. Their nomadic family, along with others from the community, moved to pastoralist reservation land given to the Maasai for settlement. The Maasai were not pastoralists, yet they needed to settle for a while and live off the crops grown on the land so they could survive the famine threatening their families, cattle, and vulnerable community members.

One unexpected bonus of this change in circumstance was the opportunity for Hannah and Grace to attend school. Although this required a four-hour walk in each direction, with a 4 a.m. start and an 8 p.m. return home, the girls were pleased to be receiving an education. It was a long, hard walk in the dark, and they only had the smoky light of a fire to assist them in completing their homework. An optional health club class was run during the lunch break. Among other things, this taught them about the illegality and health consequences of FGM.

The girls immediately planned to run away from home – Hannah choosing the refuge of her grandma, and Grace, her aunt. These women were only thirty-six and twenty-two years old, respectively, but although cut themselves, they gave their young relatives safe refuge.

In time, mediation took place between the girls and their community. Hannah and Grace had refused to go home unless they were guaranteed safety from FGM, as there were already plans in place for them to be cut. The chiefs met and guaranteed that they would be heard if they returned. The girls addressed the whole community, which decided then and there to never perform FGM again. One of the girls eventually became a teacher and the other a social worker. No girl younger than them in their community has ever been cut since.

Extraordinarily, a Maasai man there later trained as a

pastor, and many other practices were slowly addressed as a result, including child abuse and the sexual abuse of women. Change takes time, yet I never give up hope, and this story cheers my spirit in the darkest hours.

Mary Lazia

Mary Lazia was born into a relatively wealthy Maasai family in 1973. Her mother told her about FGM, a celebrated process by which Mary would become a woman when she was fourteen. Mary's mother made no mention of the negative aspects of FGM, telling her it was a harmless procedure that would bring glory and respect to her parents and herself, and that it only involved a small cut that would take a matter of days to heal.

"The most important thing to mention that my loving mother told me," says Mary, "was that a woman in Maasai society is nothing without a man to marry her, and that FGM is a promotion to that very dignified grade at which a Maasai woman shall only be able to attain self-perfection under the shelter and protection of her husband."

Mary eagerly awaited her turn to be cut, promising her parents that she would neither let them down nor cry. When the time came, however, Mary was shocked by the reality of the practice, and her eagerness turned to terror as she feared for her life. It was a month before she could leave her bed.

Mary was married at nineteen, and it was then that she began to gain an understanding of the lies she had been fed by her parents and her community. Sexual intercourse was a problem, and Mary was unable to enjoy sex throughout her marriage. She also suffered an obstructed labour and required surgical intervention to deliver her first child safely. Eventually, the shelter and protection of her husband proved wholly inadequate, as he abandoned her and their three children.

Yet Mary also came to understand that she has value beyond her relative worth to a man. Now an anti-FGM activist, she oversees alternative rite of passage ceremonies, and her own daughter's alternative ceremony was witnessed by her relatives, in-laws, and the community's elders and traditional cutters. Mary's life is a demonstration of how destructive cycles can be broken and harmful practices abolished.

Lydia

Lack of knowledge and misinformation reinforce the challenges that anti-FGM workers face. In communities that practise FGM, ignorance of its realities and taboos surrounding open discussions about female sexuality leave many women entirely uneducated about the practice until they are directly affected by it. In non-practising communities, or communities where FGM is practised on the fringes of society, the problem is commonly overlooked.

British teacher Lydia approached 28 Too Many to help ensure that teachers in Uganda had good information about FGM. She decided to sacrifice her summer holidays to help the situation in a region where her church had links.

While running her safeguarding workshop in rural south-western Uganda, she found that, of the twenty teachers in attendance, only one had any knowledge of FGM. That knowledge was based on hearsay that FGM was a medical procedure which deterred women from having extramarital sex and, as a result, prevented them from contracting HIV and AIDS.

Lydia worked with these teachers, looking in detail at the data gathered by 28 Too Many and examining the social, emotional, and physical repercussions of FGM. She taught ways to recognize girls who had been subjected to FGM before they succumbed to potential complications. The final stage of the workshop was an enthusiastic discussion about how teachers could act to eradicate FGM in their communities.

One year on from the original training, Lydia returned to the school and was pleased to see that the teachers had implemented improved policies and safety measures at the school as a result of the training. They were much more confident about starting conversations about FGM and other child safety concerns, and dealing with any related issues. In addition, they had held meetings with local leaders, parents, and others in the community to spread the message about the importance of child safety and the need to be vigilant against harmful practices such as FGM.

Further training was given to the teachers to help them promote girls' education and to help stop female students dropping out of school when they reached puberty. Plans were made to send these teachers to share the training with neighbouring schools in the county. After two years of working in the schools, the programme was launched across the country, and was subsequently scaled up to address even larger audiences.

Networking

A great deal of 28 Too Many's progress has occurred through informal networking, based on the premise that everyone needs to know about FGM. It is everyone's business to know what happens to girls in our communities. My previous HR consultancy career included coaching, and in the early days before 28 Too Many was formed I did a small amount of coaching to help friends out in their training and coaching businesses.

One early assignment was coaching a man who worked in regulatory affairs in the City. He was the neighbour of a coaching friend of mine, and I saw him for ten sessions. My friend asked me to be her daughter's godmother, and when I attended the christening I met this man's wife. She was a gynaecologist at a London teaching hospital. She had heard about my anti-FGM work from her husband and was interested. She asked if I would speak at a conference she was chairing.

The emails that followed explained that the conference was for the Institute of Psychosexual Medicine, which met twice a year. I said I would attend the upcoming conference as a psychologist and speak at the following one. That way I would get a feel for the type of talk that was needed and a handle on the audience. The first conference was on the psychological impact of cancer, and as I had cared for my parents, who had both died of cancer, I could easily relate to the topic. The second was tailored to my experience, and was therefore promoted as a cross-cultural focus. I spoke on FGM and another speaker addressed issues relating to homosexuality in different countries. This was one of the first opportunities for me to address several hundred medical practitioners, and the organizers decided to feature the content in the institute's professional journal over two issues. This, in turn, led to more contacts and further speaking engagements. A raft of opportunities stemmed from a few informal networking relationships.

I also gave talks to gatherings of medics at a West London Mental Health Trust and a hospital grand round in Kent, which was an ongoing professional development event. One of my reasons for learning basic fistula surgery in Nigeria and basic midwifery in Pakistan was to be able to hold my own with these audiences. My psychology training was also invaluable in explaining the PTSD, depression, and anxiety associated with FGM.

At the other end of the spectrum of talks, I was often called on to speak to audiences from the Mothers' Union, Women's Institute, Soroptimists and Zonta; all women's groups committed to faith-based or secular action with the aim of improving the lot of women around the world. I would be asked to deliver speeches at after-dinner events in London, at conferences, and at women's weekends away from churches across the country.

As our presence has grown on the web, we have been contacted by an increasingly diverse audience. From the early days, I would speak to different groups every two weeks. That number grew to about 100 talks delivered annually to audiences of between ten and 10,000. Over the years, this has given me the opportunity to train and speak to nearly 100,000 people – all of whom are influencers in their environments, communities, and areas of work. This is in addition to people on the bus or the tube, at family gatherings, hospital appointments, drinks parties, and more. I have started to say "I will impact every dinner party" or "Make sure the person I sit next to has a strong stomach" before attending social events. I had one farmer ask exactly what FGM was and insist that I draw the anatomy out on a napkin. Then there was a man in Africa who grabbed my plastic laminated visual aid of the four types of FGM and hold it up like an umbrella over his head in an attempt to understand the anatomy three-dimensionally!

Whoever we are networking with, two of our key strategies at 28 Too Many are to influence influencers and to empower local organizations to help end FGM through knowledge and training resources. Both involve sharing the key points of our research, stories of hope, and knowledge of what works here and elsewhere. My aims have been to influence religious leaders and heads of faith bodies, including archbishops of the Church of England, the Pope, Muslim imams, bishops of the Anglican Communion, and a number of first ladies.

We were contacted by the policy office of the Church of England, which wanted us to deliver some training to its policy officers. We had been recommended by Restored, and we delivered a half-day workshop to around thirty attendees. This is just the type of audience we want to train, as these people influence the Church of England's social policy in the UK and possibly also the wider Anglican communion, which covers many of our twenty-eight target countries.

While I was there, I asked a women's officer how I could speak at General Synod, the Church of England policy-setting event that happens annually in London or York. She seemed to think it was perfectly possible, and after a few months of correspondence I found myself on the way to York.

As I emerged from the station, I discovered it was a race day and felt underdressed without heels, a frothy dress, and a fascinator! However, I caught the bus to the university and went to check in. It was a large complex and synod had taken over the whole place. People tended to sit in cliques, perhaps reconnecting from previous parish roles or ordination training.

I had managed to obtain a three-day pass so I could sit in and see synod pass its decisions. The first decision concerned female clergy clothing guidelines. Other similarly important topics followed!

I had a seminar slot at the fringe event, and before my 6 p.m. session I wandered around the marketplace of stalls. I was scheduled at the same time as dinner, as all the fringe events were – given that the business of synod was the key priority for attendees. FGM is a challenging subject to speak on at the best of times, but even more so at synod, where many from the more conservative end of the Christian spectrum represent their views. I was very pleased to see the familiar face of Elaine Storkey at my session. As she was an author on violence against women issues, and chair of Restored, I was very pleased and honoured by her attendance. I was also pleased to meet other people who were committed to our cause and would be allies on the journey.

At an event in Devon, I was shocked to hear the story of a missionary who had been raped in Africa, become pregnant, and eventually had her baby back in the UK. Her mixed-race child was refused a place at day care and she was told, "We don't take black children here." I was horrified to hear this in 2011 and reported it to someone who could take the necessary action.

As a mission worker myself, and a long-term worker in HR, I am often horrified but rarely surprised by anything these days. However, being asked to judge and award chocolates to the winner of a floral art competition at the Women's Institute meeting in Devon before I spoke on FGM did surprise me – and it was certainly a new experience!

The next day I was asked to teach the teachers at a large secondary school, and to teach in various religious studies, and philosophy and ethics classes – all with no warning! Trips like this make good use of my time, especially if I can leave resources for others to use, enabling the work to carry on once we have gone. I would love to have a UK team dedicated to training others. The demand is there, just not the resource... yet!

The United Nations

A particularly key period of networking came in 2012. The Inspired Individual scholarship, British Citizenship Award, and charity launch had raised the profile of 28 Too Many. As a result, I was able to attend seminars at the United Nations in Geneva in October 2012 and later in New York, where I managed to lobby and have an impact on the state of FGM.

We were granted UN Economic and Social Council (ECOSOC) status via our relationship with Tearfund and Restored, which meant we could speak, share, write, attend meetings, and have an influence by voting at UN-hosted events. Geneva was host to the European NGOs under the National Alliance of Women's Organizations (NAWO), and acted as a focused gathering for 500 NGOs to meet and agree on a set of motions. These would be put forward to the full Commission on the Status of Women (CSW) in New York the following March.

The other caucuses from the Asia Pacific group were to meet in Bangkok, Thailand; from Africa in Addis Ababa, Ethiopia; from South America in Santiago, Chile; from North America in New York, USA; and from the Middle East in Lebanon. Each group had representation to meet and hear from the other caucuses.

I knew around twenty participants in Geneva and was pleased to have attended plenty of NAWO meetings in London. Before going to Geneva, I had been invited to parliament as one of six to represent the NAWO non-governmental organization consortium. I was fascinated to learn that there were three groupings of countries: warm to our views (including Scandinavia, Canada, and Belgium); cool to our views (including the USA, Vatican City, and Poland); and cold to our views (including Russia, Palestine, Iran, Iraq, and Afghanistan). The UK government was meeting with its fellow warm countries to agree strategies of working, collaborating, brokering, and voting together. We knew the cold countries were doing the same.

The cool countries were being courted by the hot and the cold countries. We heard of hotel gatherings in the west-US desert being hosted for Arabic and African audiences, offering their guests female company and access to alcohol while listening to country standpoints. The cold countries often voted as a bloc – thus blocking progress on the rights of women, Convention on the Elimination of all Forms of Discrimination Against Women (CEDAW) principles, and SDGs.[16] Far from just maintaining the status quo, they actively aimed to reduce the reproductive, human, educational, economic, and health rights of women. I heard of some extraordinary tactics proposed to affect voting, including the delivery of pizza to a closed session so that the voting could be rigged by pizza delivery personnel, who were really lobbyists!

I attended meetings on youth voice, on education, on the role of men and boys, on health and harmful practices, and on economic empowerment. I asked a question about FGM at each session and compiled a written statement of 28 Too Many's wishes. I also managed to ask a question in the main session. Wearing a red jacket helped to ensure that I was picked out from more than 600 activists and was able to ask my question!

I had been staying at the John Knox University accommodation for Christian workers, which was affordable and also close to the UN. I travelled there by bus each day with two nuns from New York, both of whom had been seconded to the UN. At seventy years old, one was told that she was too young to go to a nuns' care home. That will be me one day, I hope! The week was intense, long, and focused, and it involved tactical and work meetings. I went to one fancy dinner venue, where the nuns and I ate soup and the cheapest dishes, as our budgets did not match the UN's. It's always easy to spot faith workers and NGOs!

With plenty of work done, yet more to do, I left Geneva feeling that FGM and forced marriage would be firmly on

---

16 CEDAW is an international treaty adopted by the United Nations General Assembly in 1979. For more on Sustainable Development Goals, see www.28toomany.org/thematic/the-sustainable-development-goals-and-fgm.

the agenda for New York in March. By the time March came, I negotiated hard and won what I called a golden ticket from Tearfund's allowance of ten to represent Tearfund, go to the opening ceremony, and speak at the UN main events.

I went to the preparation and training day on a Sunday, having flown to New York on the Saturday. On the Saturday evening, I met up with Dr Katie Gentile, whose doctoral thesis was based on the diaries I had written during my adolescence and thirties. She later published a book, and I learned a great deal from that collaboration. She was speaking at a psychotherapists' party, so I attended as her guest and quite enjoyed myself in another of my worlds, introduced as "Dr Wilson: a psychologist visiting from London to speak at the UN on FGM".

Back to reality, and my minuscule pod hotel near the UN area, I was woken by rubbish collections early the next morning and got up to see if any of the four bathrooms were available. This was followed by a run at around 6 a.m. in slushy, grey snow, and a take-out breakfast of juice, muesli, and hot tea before changing and heading off to the UN. Not quite the jet-set lifestyle my fellow guests from the previous evening might have imagined.

The day's events lasted until early evening: large, formal morning sessions in Salon I or II – or in overflow tents if seats were gone; themed afternoon caucus meetings; and NGO seminars from 10 a.m. to 7 p.m. in hour-long slots. I was involved in delivering two with Veena of Tearfund: one presentation on our FGM work, and one, in collaboration with other speakers on how the Christian faith is against FGM. There were also plenty of events hosted by the United Nations Children's Fund (UNICEF), the United Nations Population Fund (UNFPA), the World Health Organization (WHO), and others – all at their own New York buildings. This meant plenty of running around the city. I invited my cousin to attend a talk and film-clip screening on FGM, which was somewhat graphic. I don't like showing overly graphic material, as I feel it can be re-traumatizing, but she said it was appropriate for an American audience. I still had to shut my eyes to some of the images.

Early each morning, thirty to fifty of us met as a UK NGO group at the New York City Baha'i Center to discuss the activities we were attending, the talks we were giving, and who we were targeting for advocacy campaigns. We then scattered, before later regrouping at the headquarters of the UK ambassador to debrief and share findings about how the cold and cool countries were moving. Attendance from the ambassadorial country reps was patchy at the main talks, and only a quarter of the attendees had voting rights. These were the key people in terms of our voting intentions. Many had diplomatic status and were lured away by the shopping opportunities New York had to offer, with wives especially filling up extra diplomatic luggage!

I was amazed to see an array of empty seats in the main hall and used the opportunity to sit in one of them. I wasn't really aware of the protocol – that as an observer I was meant to sit 150 rows back in the cheap seats. I sat in the Zimbabwean row, but at least I didn't use the microphone to represent another nation! I could have attended the opening ceremony, but went to collect some materials instead – thus missing a special moment in the voting chamber. Another year, maybe. The art that filled UN buildings and gardens – often gifts from other state visits – was stunning. We had one lunch in the garden and one dinner reception at the UK ambassador's home.

The main purpose of attending was to ensure that FGM featured in the closing document. That way, all NGOs and activists could lobby to make sure that governments committed resources to this issue. My strategy was to bring it up at all the seminars I attended, write down my views formally in each seminar, hold seminars myself, ask pertinent questions at key events, and hand cards and literature out to key dignitaries. I felt tired yet satisfied after seven days of intense work. Before we left, I met my cousin and a Restored colleague in New York and visited a couple of sights I had not seen before, including a footpath made from old sleepers and Ground Zero.

Returning home, I felt the event had been well worth attending. It took a week to see what the parliamentarians would action in the second week, but they ratified our suggested statements, amending them in response to pressure from home influences, civil service aides, and personal agendas. I eventually saw the final agreed form of words – and was amazed and horrified to see that while early child and forced marriage was listed as a new category of harmful practice, FGM had not been included at all. I emailed the National Alliance of Women's Organizations NGO coordinator and then later the chair of all the sessions I had attended. Finally, I sent an email to the senior civil servant from the Government Equality Office and copied in the Department for International Development minister, Lynne Featherstone.

After a week of emails and a flurry of activity, I received an email confirming that this had been an accidental omission introduced at the editing stage. I am still sceptical about this. However, the important thing is that those three small letters are now in the document, and therefore in the Sustainable Development Goals. This is one of my greatest achievements; an area of FGM that I have personally impacted.

Working with DFID

In early 2014, we started working with the Department for International Development (DFID), as we were considered a trusted voice in the FGM sector. I was invited at short notice to a DFID meeting on faith and FGM. There were four of us in the room, and I understood that a Muslim organization had been asked to gather the names of faith leaders who had agreed to sign a pledge saying no to FGM. I asked how many names had been collected and was told they only had fifteen! I was amazed at this small number, as my CMS newsletter had a circulation of at least 1,000. I ambitiously said I could collect several hundred, and they seemed very pleased.

The deadline was short, and the pledge had to be kept secret. We couldn't use social media to promote this, and we needed a wet-ink signature on a pledge of four sentences with wording that I did not consider to be finalized! As the deadline approached, it was extended for us to collect signatures against forced marriage as well. We got to work and used all our networks and networking skills, achieving a list of more than 350 names by the cut-off date.

Meanwhile, we were invited to pitch for a spotlight seminar at the UK government and UNICEF's first Girl Summit in 2014, and were chosen as one of fourteen organizations. We were also encouraged to bring a charity partner to the UK to attend alongside us, so we invited Revd Dr Medad Birungi, the pastor in charge of World Shine Ministries, with whom Lydia had taught and shared her safeguarding training. Dr Medad's work had grown from twenty teachers to twenty schools to 900-plus leaders. Each participant needed a vetted four-minute speech, so we wrote mine and his. We produced a PowerPoint presentation for him, sorted out his accommodation and flight, and obtained a travel grant for him to attend (along with his wife, whose costs he paid – though she went shopping in London while the summit was in progress!).

We met DFID minister Lynne Featherstone at the summit and presented our pledges to her and other ministers. I was spotted by friends on the 6 p.m. news, so I had plenty of texts that night. We were also acknowledged by Deputy Prime Minister Nick Clegg for having achieved our faith leaders' pledge, and as one of the successes in ending FGM. I felt proud of all the work that had gone into this project. I had even sent the pledge to the archbishops of Canterbury and York, having met Justin Welby at Canterbury Cathedral during a service to mark an African link to CMS's history and John Setamu at General Synod. I very cheekily accosted them both – and though they *never* sign pledges, both agreed to signed ours. I was very proud to have these names on the sheet, and I knew my parents would also have been.

The Girl Summit took place on 22nd July 2014, and was the first international forum to look at FGM and child early forced marriage (CEFM). It focused on sharing successful approaches and securing new commitments from governments, civil society, faith leaders, and the private sector to take action on these issues.

The three main aims were:

- To share what works: learning and celebrating success through sessions on particular approaches or aspects of combatting FGM and CEFM.
- To agree an agenda for change: securing commitments to action through a charter that governments and other attendees would sign up to.
- To engage people for change: inspiring a generation to declare their support in ending CEFM and FGM.

As an organization dedicated to researching and campaigning to end FGM, 28 Too Many supported the summit's aims and we were pleased that this high-profile event brought attention to, and raised awareness of, the terrible impact of FGM and CEFM.

The UK government hoped the summit would be the catalyst for a step change, encouraging many more activists to engage in a global movement. It highlighted the changes taking place in communities such as the Maasai village in Kenya we visited, where Hannah and Grace had learned about FGM at a school health club, running away when they learned about their impending FGM. Ultimately, those two girls inspired a whole village to abandon the practice, and the summit intended to inspire others to end FGM and CEFM worldwide. The desire to create a world in which FGM and CEFM are no longer practised is an ambitious one. It can only be achieved when girls' and women's rights are respected so they can fulfil their potential, free from violence and discrimination.

We continue to have a close relationship with DFID, which cites our research as one of the reasons for its focus on FGM and its £35 million grant to help end the practice. We are also members of a number of other organizations and groups, including the Home Office-led FGM Forum, the FGM community group at health and wellbeing charity Manor Garden, the Gender and Development Network (GADN), and the National Association of Women's Organizations (NAWO). More recently, we have made links with the Metropolitan Police's faith, FGM, and witchcraft expert group, Child Abuse Linked to Faith or Belief (CALFB).

We have been pleased to see an increase in the engagement of men and boys in the campaign to end FGM. Their role is crucial, as men hold much of the power, status, money, and leadership in marriages, homes, villages, and communities, yet historically they know very little about FGM.

There has also been a huge move to engage the youth voice. Since 2005, when I first became involved in anti-FGM work, I have seen a generation of health professionals with whom I initially worked retiring from their health roles, and their children or grandchildren becoming the first generations to not be cut. Engaging these young people can make all the difference. For example, Integrate Bristol – a charity set up to end FGM and empower young people – has grown to become Integrate UK, and the first girls it helped are now doing master's courses at university, having lobbied Michael Gove and others. A new generation of fourteen-year-olds is now continuing the work.

Ethiopia

After a trip to Ethiopia in 2012 to launch our Ethiopia country report, I visited the world-famous fistula hospital in Addis Ababa, which was started by Australian obstetrician and gynaecologist Dr Catherine Hamlin. It had taken me six months to obtain a proper meeting, as people are usually only allowed a thirty-minute tour. I wanted a proper visit so I could ask about the correlation between FGM and fistula, and why the hospital never discussed this. I believed it was due to its sensitive links with certain faith groups that informally promoted FGM.

I met with Dr Hamlin, who was by then in her nineties, and was given a private tour of Desdemende, a community for people who have undergone at least two attempts at fistula correction. As the procedures had failed for them, the women were rehoused within a closed community, where they had beautiful housing, medical supplies, food, training, and work. I found it sad that their husbands and families would visit at the weekend, yet these women never left. I often wondered about the complex reasons that prevented them from returning home permanently, although it was clear that the economic benefits made them want to remain. I believe the donor base of the United States Agency for International Development (USAID) and the USA have a responsibility to address this if reintegration is the goal of corrective surgery and failed fistula rehabilitation.

Kenya

A couple of years after launching our Kenya report, I was invited to give a talk on FGM at a conference in Bondo, Kenya, run by Domnic (a fellow Inspired Individual scholar) and his Ekklesia Foundation. It was a privilege to speak on gender, the biblical model of equality, and the cultural issues behind FGM. Many of my other Inspired Individual colleagues from South Africa, Kenya, Tanzania, and Uganda were there, and we used the time around the conference to receive training on strategy, founder syndrome, and leadership. As we had all birthed and run organizations, we needed to know when to pass these organizations on to others, and how.

In 2015, 28 Too Many took part in a trip to the central Maasai area of Kenya with a team from Cricket Without Boundaries (CWB). This CWB team had worked in around six African countries, teaching cricket to help communicate about safe sex and the prevention of HIV and AIDS. After ten years, they asked the Maasai which was the next topic that needed addressing, and the universal response was FGM. As CWB didn't know much about the practice, we were asked to deliver a teaching day in Coventry to the team visiting Kenya, and to devise a trial on FGM reduction, which could then be rolled out as a programme in other countries if successful. A colleague and I made a training module for the training day, and for the community training of junior and senior schoolchildren, health practitioners, educators, social workers, paralegals, community elders, the police, court officials, and the church.

Taking part in this trip was a huge privilege. We stayed at a game lodge in rural plateau Kenya, a ninety-minute coach journey from the schools we were visiting. I flew with the club team of eleven women and one man. We had all collected donated cricket kit – bats, balls, and so on – and I had been given cricket lessons by my vicar on the lawn outside church! I also took his bat and ball with me. Although my only other bat and ball skills had been learned from school rounders, the bat was very useful for keeping order in a class of 400!

On arrival in Laikipia, we collected the Maasai Cricket Warriors (MCW), who were joining us for the tour, as well as human rights lawyer and 28 Too Many volunteer, Esther. We all stayed the night at a small hotel and managed a few hours' sleep after a briefing at 8 p.m. The following morning we left at 6 a.m. It was good to be back in the land of the hot milk Milo drink, and we enjoyed *mandazi* doughnuts with a boiled egg for protein. We were honoured guests in the community, and in the usual Kenyan style a goat was killed and cooked for all the visitors and locals to eat. It was the usual chopped-up style of bone, organs, and meat in a pot, with a bit of pie covering on top. I asked if it would cause offence if I only ate the corn, and was told that was absolutely fine. Someone else was delighted to receive my meal.

The next task was to seek permission from the elders to be on their land and teach on FGM. As we walked into the area where they were sitting, they looked fierce and serious. The women were seated under one tree to the left, and the men were under another to the right. I was seated to the left of the Maasai Cricket Warriors' captain, Jonathan, a young man from the community, who was also our translator. To his right was the Cricket Without Boundaries representative, who was a Christian. In fact, half the team were believers, so we had prayed before this meeting. I had been told, "If your talk goes down badly, we'll be thrown out and sent home." No pressure! I hoped

I had covered myself by saying to Jonathan, "If you don't like what I'm saying, don't translate it!"

The meeting opened with Jonathan standing and thanking the elders. The chief nodded. After that, our CWB representative stood with a Maasai warrior and thanked the elders again, receiving another nod. Then it was over to me.

I stood, but I was only about half the height of the CWB captain! I thanked the elders, then told them a bit about myself and the team before explaining what we were there to do. I looked around at all the stern faces and suddenly felt great love and compassion. I said, "I don't even know if I have permission to speak of FGM and sexual matters in public, or in mixed company." The chief stomped his stick on the ground and said, "You have permission!" I nearly died – not only did I have permission, but it was clear that he spoke impeccable English! So on I went. At one point, I grabbed the hand of the CWB woman sitting next to me and yanked her up, saying, "We are good, chaste, godly women. We are not cut, but we are modest, and we do not need to be cut to stop us having sex."

I don't know where all this speech came from, but at the end, the chief stood, thanked us, and said we could deliver the project. Then he said to me, "Come, walk with me across my land." And that's we did… for an hour and a half! The chief had been in the police, where he had learned English, and he explained how hard it was to end FGM. Even with a 151 free dial from any phone for reports of child abuse and other issues, he explained that by the time the police got to the place where the deed was done, there was never any evidence that it had taken place or anyone there to be seen. My poor Primark pumps had not expected such a long walk, and I ended up with sore, sunburnt feet, but I also gained great insight into FGM in rural Kenya from this experience. When we got back, the coach driver was amazed to see us and couldn't believe we had walked all that way!

The trip continued well. We went to many schools and shared with more than 3,000 people in a week. The head teacher at one school had cancelled classes for the day, so more than 800 children from the age of three to sixteen were ready and willing to listen. I sent the three- to five-year-olds to do ball play and divided the five- to sixteen-year-olds between Esther and myself – each group based under an acacia tree – to train the children. We alternated ball practice and training. A 28 Too Many colleague had a nephew who worked for Rugby and Cricket UK, and had obtained six cricket sets for us to take, which was amazing. Still, it was hot, tiring work. Some of the girls who had been cut disclosed this fact to us, so we gave support and ensured follow-up. We also provided teacher packs so the schools could carry on the work once we had gone. We did some basic evaluation on a percentage of attendees by pulling some of the girls out of class and checking their before-and-after knowledge.

At the end of the trip, we attended a celebratory dinner followed by an awards ceremony. Each team member received an award. I felt I was given the best one: a chief's beaded stomping stick. We were then treated to a Maasai dance demonstration and joined in with some of the attempts at jumping, though I didn't have many height credits to help with this!

Our final day was spent visiting an FGM rescue project. This was moving, and we saw all sorts of ethical issues at play. If girls who had been rescued didn't go back home within three months, they were never reassimilated into the family. This sometimes suited the family, giving them one less mouth to feed, with overseas donors paying for their education and the girls receiving Western clothes.

We also delivered a talk at the medical centre and visited the commissioner's office, where we sought assurance that girls who disclosed FGM would be safe. He summoned the police chief, who assured us that he would protect girls and whistle-blowers. This is very important, as girls who report in some communities, or try to run away, are often scapegoated and made an example of by being subjected to a worse form of FGM than usual (Type III).

In the late afternoon, we were taken for a climb up cricket captain Jonathan's local mountain rock face. I may be short, but I am also light and plucky, so I made it up quite easily. One of the MCW men was scared of heights, so I coached him up to the top and back down. One never knows what others can or cannot do, but together we can overcome many problems!

As for outcomes, the team was pleased to have secured the support of the deputy commissioner and the head of police, which was essential for ensuring community members' ongoing participation in the programme. More than 1,750 children and young people were coached in cricket and FGM awareness through local schools, while twenty-five adults, including teachers, youth workers, and health professionals, were trained to be ongoing cricket and FGM coaches.

To round off the project, the Maasai Cricket Warriors led a celebratory day of cricket and encouraged the community to stand against FGM by declaring that their sisters and daughters would not be cut. The community committed to ending FGM and wanted to run further programmes, taking the message to neighbouring villages, including elders in a cricket seniors' team and women in a female team. They also asked us back the following year.

Later in 2015, another life highlight for me was attending the Warner Bros film premiere of *The Warriors* in Leicester Square with former Zimbabwean cricket captain Alistair Campbell and various sports dignitaries. I was subsequently interviewed on BBC Radio 4's *Woman's Hour* with the Maasai Cricket Warriors' captain, dressed in our matching red outfits!

Burkina Faso

Having made a stand in Geneva at the Europe NGO meeting, and at the main Commission on the Status of Women in New York, I had met a number of key figures. I had learned a few years earlier that there had been a personnel change at the top of the Inter-African Committee (IAC), and had been pleased to meet the new head of this important organization, Dr Morissanda Kouyaté. When I first heard of the IAC's role – a group of twenty-eight countries committed to ending FGM and other harmful practices – I hoped it could host our research database/information portal and enable us to connect with the key players in each country. For some reason, this function has never been fully realized. That said, the IAC is usually present at key meetings, even though many other NGOs do not consider them important enough to attend.

I heard an IAC meeting was being held in Burkina Faso in 2014 and decided it would be a great opportunity to attend and meet all the IAC country representatives in one visit. The key dignitaries, ministers, speakers, and Girl Generation representatives (the communications brand for the DFID's £35 million FGM project) stayed at a smart hotel in the centre of the city. Based on my aid work experience, I needed to decide whether to stay there so I could network informally outside the sessions, or whether I should stay down the road in much more modest accommodation. I decided on the latter and asked my Tearfund friends to help by arranging a taxi to pick me up from the airport.

I bumped into an NGO colleague who had missed the airport transport, so we gave her a lift into the city. It was an early start the next day, and it seemed the pick-up did not go from my hotel, so I needed help getting to my venue, especially as it wasn't clear whether I should be going to the hotel or the conference venue. By the time we got to the hotel, we had missed the shuttle bus. I was hot, tired, stressed, and a little emotional by this point – and it was only 8 a.m.! Lovely as it was, my hotel seemed to have only a few visitors like me paying a day rate. It seemed to cater more for an hourly clientele, particularly on a Saturday night. It was the hot, rainy season, and one of my evening meals was a washout owing to a big African storm, during which tables and chairs were scattered in the wind and red rain fell, covering the white metal tables in a pox-like rash. I sat outside and watched the night customers come and go!

On the last day of the conference, we were offered the chance to visit an orphanage and a witch village. I am not keen on orphanages as a model for accommodating children whose parents have died, or who are unable or unwilling to take care of them. It made me uncomfortable to be paraded in front of the children, who were often deprived of love and human contact, with few staff looking after them.

During my time in Nairobi, a few of us women from our Medair house went to an orphanage after church each Sunday to feed children whose mothers had left them behind in hospital after giving birth, often because the babies had been conceived through rape. I wanted to give the children some love and warm bodily contact so they would learn how to form some sort of positive attachment before returning home or going to stay with relatives or foster carers, but it was a bittersweet experience. I also had an uncomfortable experience seeing the recipients of Operation Christmas Child in Belarus, run by Samaritan's Purse. One donor couple had wanted an ongoing annual relationship with a child in an orphanage – buying her pink trainers and an anorak. Tragically, the beneficiary was roughed up by the other children in her dormitory one night as the others had not received any extras. As is common in orphanages, clothing was held communally, so the child never even wore the outfit.

I reluctantly headed to the orphanage in Burkina Faso and then to the witch village, which made me equally uncomfortable. We were ushered into a large room for a short introduction about the background of these alleged witches. Around 450 accused women were living in this village, and there were ten other witch villages in the country. Sometimes a young male child would be banished along with his mother. I counted seven boys in the room that day.

Hearing their stories made me feel angry and sad, as these successful women had run their own businesses, owned homes, and were wives and mothers, yet they had literally been run out of their villages by their accusers. Complex emotions lay behind these cases, often including jealousy between wives over the birth of a child or a successful entrepreneurial venture; or there because of a rivalry over age, beauty, or perceived favouritism.

Sometimes a woman would be accused of a suspicious death and the corpse would be carried around the village until the spirits "showed" who was guilty. The accused woman was then chased out of the village. The challenge is that, once accused, it is difficult to obtain justice. Proving one's innocence is often as impossible as the ancient ways of identifying a witch. The way a beheaded chicken lands often seals the individual's fate: facing up she is guilty, facing down she is a liar.

Various charities supported these supposed witches to start over again, and in many cases there had been some level of reconciliation with their families. Often the husbands and children would come to visit and eat with them, and on occasion the chief would allow them to return home. Although many hope to see an end to this practice, it will only stop when the chiefs decide this is in their best interest.

My last formal day at the conference enabled me to meet all the IAC country coordinators. I wore my best waxed Nigerian dress, rattled off a couple of lines in English or French to each delegate, and swapped business cards. I hoped this would make our task of researching each country considerably easier, and it did help in some cases.

There was an envelope for each of us in the briefcases we had been given for our conference papers, and inside was a golden ticket that we were told not to lose. It was a special invitation to a reception at the home of the First Lady, Chantal Compaoré. She often travelled with her husband, and had visited the White House and the UK. She had also written an article for *The Guardian* in November 2014, shortly after I was in Uganda, commending the Egyptian and Ugandan presidents' stances on FGM and asking for more to be done in Africa. I walked up the red carpet with the others and personally met her. She had two plush thrones, though we both stood after I had curtseyed. After that, we sat around a swimming pool eating a sumptuous meal, listening to live music, and watching the dancing. As I headed back to my basic hotel room, which was very noisy, being a Saturday night, the disparity between rich and poor within the aid world challenged me, as it always did.

A matter of months later, I woke up one morning to hear on the radio that there had been a coup, and that the president and first lady had fled the country nearly thirty years after the coup that had brought them to power. Although now residing in

Côte d'Ivoire, I have since met the former first lady while she was visiting Europe, and she still has a passion to end the practice.

The campaign against FGM in Burkina Faso has not progressed as much as I had hoped since our visit. Reflecting on this, I realize that ending FGM in Africa is a precarious process, and it will take time to see real and lasting change.

West Africa

Another highlight for me was the trip mentioned earlier to West Africa in 2015. We headed to Senegal first, then on to the Gambia before I travelled to Mali on my own, launching the relevant report in each country.

We stayed with a Dutch couple in Senegal who only had two rooms and made all our meals for us. We went to see their work with disadvantaged children while we were there. I had to give an impromptu talk in French to a team of FGM campaigners, which was a bit of a challenge. Thank goodness we had summarized the findings of our Senegal report in French! We had four meetings a day, as well as attending a conference, so we had a taxi driver to take us around. This is always a stressful negotiation: how many dollars will it cost? Is petrol on top? Are any supplements or tips needed because of traffic? Are any meals included? I always ask someone to recommend a driver, yet often it still ends in stress.

I was pleased to meet representatives from Tostan,[17] DFID, and various other organizations in Senegal. We also delivered a training session to thirty women in a rural village via a translator. The translator giggled when I mentioned the word "clitoris", which she then had to translate!

All too soon it was time to leave for a week in the Gambia. It felt edgier there, as unchaperoned women were not welcome in public, which reminded me of Nigeria. We had our own apartment, so we bought enough food to make a couple of

---

17 An Africa-based organization working directly with rural communities leading their own development. See www.tostan.org.

meals, and some snacks, bananas, and bread for lunch on the road. One meeting took place in a fancy hotel, where we had a good coffee by the pool, in sight of the beach. I even wandered down and put my feet, which had become bruised and black, in the sea.

We wrote a news update for Facebook each day and a weekly blog. That always felt like a great victory, given the difficult environment and lack of reliable infrastructure and Wi-Fi! We had a free day with no appointments on a Sunday, so my companion and I went back to the posh hotel and asked how we could go about hiring a boat. It wasn't tourist season, so we found it easy to secure a booking. Three men took us out on an exclusive two-hour sea trip. It felt quite safe, though one can never be sure. We saw beautiful wildlife, birds, trees, mangrove swamps, and much more. All felt well with our world.

On our last full day in the Gambia, we visited a newspaper and they asked if they could record an interview about our work. The next day, there it was – an A3 article, word for word what I had said!

After this, it was time for my companion to head home. I said goodbye to her at the airport entrance, as only passengers could enter the terminal building. The departures screen was broken, and not knowing where to go she sadly missed her plane home. So she came back to our apartment, we remade her bed, and she left the following day after I had headed off to Mali. Travel in Africa!

I stayed with very close friends and their children in Mali. We had been at All Nations Christian College together, and Gemma is our 28 Too Many Mali country coordinator (the equivalent of Esther in Kenya and Richard in Uganda). The weekend was fun, as I went to Gemma's birthday party at a smart restaurant and had a chance to dress up. I had only taken West African clothes with me, so I was delighted to share her Western outfits. Gemma's daughter was very curious about the plaster covering my biopsy incision, and they prayed for my health.

We were also pleased to meet UNICEF for a meal meeting, and they agreed to host the first NGO gathering – a major step forward. We met the chairs of many organizations and heard some of the reasons why the FGM situation had remained stagnant. It was rumoured that a very high-ranking politician was opposed to backing anti-FGM legislation in Mali. This is why the NGO gathering was so important, as it meant people would see what they *could* do, not what they *couldn't* do.

As well as shared buses, we also sometimes experienced shared taxis, as others would simply jump in and join us. As she was eight months pregnant, I sat Gemma on the window side of the taxi on one occasion, while I was shoved into the middle seat next to a rather smelly young man. All of a sudden, this young man vomited down my arm! I think he had been drinking alcohol. I helped Gemma out, then followed after her, pouring water over my arm. Annoyingly, we had to pay for the taxi all the way home, even though we hadn't arrived at our destination. We continued our journey on foot, so as not to cause a row over twenty pence, even if it was unjust. People have died in London for less, and at this point it was about breathing in and letting go of the small stuff.

Rome

One of the most surprising and enjoyable trips of this last decade was the one when I met Pope Francis! I had gone with a colleague from Germany to Rome to represent the IAC and to attend an End FGM conference in Rome. We shared our medicalization paper, spoke to many of the key contacts from forthcoming country reports, and met with activists from the UK, Europe, and across the globe. It was interesting to see what progress was being made in terms of unnecessary surgery in the case of intersex children, in male genital mutilation (MGM), and in FGM within same-sex unions in some African countries. We worked hard all day at the conference before heading to a dinner. Having attended the pre-dinner at a key donor's property and working hard to secure a seat at the table, I was interested to see who was and who wasn't on the guest list.

The following day I headed to the Pope's audience with a companion and my colleague. I had written and faxed a couple of times, but hadn't understood how to access my special audience ticket. As it was, our seats were upgraded to the fifth row, so we were sitting with nuns from his area of Buenos Aires. I really wanted to speak to him and felt I couldn't just leave without doing so. In fact, I felt my feet stick to the floor! I prayed and felt God say, "Look at the ceiling! The paraplegic was lowered from the roof!"

I went to the last but one row and stood at the aisle end, hoping he might come back up the aisle he had entered through. After an hour or so, he criss-crossed the aisle, greeting a baby on the right, a young girl on the left, and a mother and child on the right. Then he crossed the aisle to hold my hand and speak with me. I couldn't believe it! Out of 6,000 people, I was one of under 100 people to meet him that day, and one of only four in the general audience. Amazingly, an article about our meeting later appeared in *Inside the Vatican* magazine, containing several of my quotes and affirming his blessing on my ministry to end FGM. It really was a miracle. I felt that if this could happen, anything could!

EIGHT:
LIVING WITH CANCER

I guess it was to be expected that my diagnosis would have an impact on 28 Too Many. Having said that, I was most challenged in this area. The charity had been in existence since 2010, but was only registered in 2012, so when my health crisis struck we were only officially three years old as a charity. At the July 2015 board meeting I asked the board to step up while I was having treatment. My deputy was also asked to step up, and in an ideal world these plans would have carried the charity through this difficult period. I was available for consultations throughout, and had agreed to meet my PA and operations manager weekly to see what action, advice, or resourcing was needed.

Unfortunately, stepping up was not on everyone's agenda, and the first person to step back was my deputy, who went on her summer holidays and never returned to the charity. Her health had also been a challenge, and in hindsight perhaps I shouldn't have given her more authority and responsibility. I had been coaching a chair-designate over a period of six months to replace me as chair at our October AGM, and I discussed this news with her. She decided to implement an organizational review – something I never would have suggested during a time of change. In fact, we had been offered a pro bono review by one of our charity ambassadors, but I thought it would be better to undertake it once some stability had returned. However, the review went ahead with a consultant recommended by our vice-chair. All team members were interviewed, including me. The atmosphere was strange, to the point where I wondered whether the consultant wanted my CEO role, as she was looking for a post. She is now the CEO of a charity, in fact. I later talked to the vice-chair about her recommendation, and she agreed the consultant had not been the right person for this scenario.

Our communications manager, volunteer finance manager, and fundraising consultant all decided to move on – to look after parents, to retire, or to take on new roles – so the team was swiftly shrinking. One of our board members had found the Summer Away Day a challenge and had also chosen to leave. We looked to replace board members in pairs to maintain around ten to twelve. Each brought something to the charity for a season, yet things were constantly changing and we needed a safe, stable team in this unsettled time when I was unable to be as visible as I would have liked. My PA had been facing some personal issues after her father died from cancer. Having worked for me for around twelve years, she left the charity before Christmas. This was very sad, but it meant that I had my home back to myself as I recovered from my treatment.

Appointed in October 2015, the new chair left four months later in February 2016 – the night before a special board meeting at which we had planned to agree to implement the consultant's report (which had been brought to the January board meeting). The chair, vice-chair, consultant, and I met the night before to see the report. The consultant had included some very critical opinions without any data to back it up. As I went home, I wondered how we had got to this place. I rang a few board members, as I was concerned that I might lose my job. The board meeting was extremely challenging, but in the end the experience brought us all closer together. Once again, I felt there was a better future ahead. We appointed the vice-chair, who was also Restored's chair and my main contact at CMS, as acting CEO.

We faced one other exceptionally challenging staffing situation, which involved a clash of opinions, unpleasant accusations, and very strained relationships. I remember having caught an infection and being too unwell for chemo that February. My friend had driven me to her house for a week of antibiotics and recovery, with treatment at Dorset Cancer Centre and plenty of TLC. While resting in Dorset, I received a call from the vice-chair to apologetically say, "There's a problem with your expenses." My heart dropped and I spent much of the next day crying. I felt my honesty was being called into question by the treasurer, as though I were being accused of deliberately misappropriating funds. I really questioned whether I wanted to carry on, yet I felt I had done nothing wrong. I certainly didn't need the added adrenaline and cortisol swirling round my body alongside the chemo drugs – and this whole difficult period rekindled many painful situations from the past for me. I am sad to say that it took us eighteen months to sort the issue out, after endless meetings, new contracts, and a lot of wasted time and energy. CMS handled the situation excellently, and thankfully we have now moved into a new season.

One helpful development during this challenging season was being able to bring my old Inspired mentor, Sean, on board. It was either a spot of synchronicity or God's hand, as he was in the UK, away from his German home, and just happened to be looking for work. I had an immediate need for a part-time operations manager, so I asked him to help me realize the legacy and vision of my charity: the twenty-eight country reports and the 10:10:10 vision. As we had worked together for four years, we already knew each other well and trusted one another to share the organization's leadership and management. He is still with us on an annual rolling contract, playing a key operations role while I focus on vision, strategy, speaker engagements, and fundraising.

Cancer buddies

My health has remained fairly stable over the four years since I received my diagnosis, despite the initial infection, a couple of trips to A&E, and the week I spent at my friend's house when I became neutropenic and my white blood cell count was too low for chemotherapy.

In July 2016 I joined a cancer survivors' writing group held every Thursday at University College London Hospital (UCLH). I had moved the care I was due to be given at Barnet General Hospital to UCLH quite early on, except for A&E visits and blood tests. UCLH is an excellent hospital and I feel I am in good hands there.

Around a year after my treatment began, a friend from the writing group, who had ovarian cancer, told me her chemo buddy had suddenly become very ill. I offered to go with her to see her friend after our group, as she was upset. As soon as I saw this friend, it struck me that she was critically ill and probably dying. She had a very enlarged stomach and there was a smell that made me feel as though something wasn't right. She was in a cubicle with her son, being sick. I offered to pray, which seemed to calm her down. Then we spoke to her husband, who was sitting outside the cubicle, for an hour or so. The nursing sister later said he had been forced to take her out of the cubicle in order to have her readmitted via A&E so she could be put on a ward... What a crazy system!

Over the next couple of days, I supported my friend in various ways – including providing links to end-of-life hospice care and advice, and on how to share bad news with family members. I also googled "stage four ovarian cancer" and found a Cancer Research UK (CRUK) statistic which revealed that only 5% of people with the condition live for more than a year. My heart sank, as she had been diagnosed fourteen months earlier. She died four days after our visit. As I looked at the CRUK chart, I inadvertently saw my own prognosis. It didn't give me as long as I had hoped.

I talked to a couple of friends for support, and had a coffee with the clinical nurse specialist at Cherry Lodge Cancer Care in Barnet, where I had acupuncture and attended a lymphoma support group every six weeks. Her advice was that prognosis is never very accurate and should not be sought or given. Yet how could I unknow what I knew? I took her advice and discussed it with my oncologist at the next month's meeting. He gave me a "half-empty" view of my prognosis. Six months later, and after a couple of late appointment cancellations on his part, I saw his superior, the director. I said that I planned to change consultant once my intense chemo was over because I didn't like the half-empty approach. He offered me an immediate swap and even agreed to tell the consultant on my behalf – an offer that was too good to refuse! The tipping point had come when he said I wasn't well enough for the last chemo cycle. I argued that it was the only thing keeping me in remission before I received further treatment. I won this battle, but was pleased to move to a more philosophical, "half-full" consultant for the remainder of the long and difficult journey.

My friend's friend was the first in my cancer network to die. I have subsequently lost four precious friends from the writing group, two from my photography group at North London Hospice, and two from my home church. Losing eight friends to cancer was compounded by the deaths of more friends who died from other causes, and those I see dying in my hospice role. Many are young, and it brings my own mortality into focus each time I walk along this path, attend the funeral, and meet the family I have heard so much about.

All of this reminds me that time is short, that there is much still to do, and that this is not the season for rest. Yet often I am torn between being too busy and having the feeling that I may never return somewhere or see someone again. This needs prayerful wisdom to balance, as my closest friends feel I do too much – which I do! – yet others think I am fine now, believing the Facebook projections of who I am. Of course, like most people, I mainly post positive things.

Post-cancer challenges

One of the challenges of my post-cancer season has been liaising with the various management structures in my life. CMS has been excellent as the umbrella sending agency that looks after my welfare as a mission partner. A year or so after receiving my diagnosis, I moved from the Africa team to the North Africa, Middle East, and Europe team so I could more easily attend the alternate year gatherings and have closer support from the personnel team, led by the head of HR. That said, my Africa team line and personnel manager came to visit me while I was having chemo and undergoing home-based isolation to avoid infection, bringing flowers. We had a long tea with the supportive vice-chair of 28 Too Many, who had taken on responsibility for my pastoral care, appraisal, and wellbeing. Until this point, I had worked a sixty-hour week, yet I only had a contract for three days, so I was paid for just twenty-one hours, which amounted to £15,000. In reality, I received much less than this once National Insurance, admin fees, pension, and other costs had been taken into account. I had to raise my own support, and was worried about raising enough for myself and 28 Too Many if I were paid more.

As I was unwell, my vice-chair insisted that my allowance be increased to a full-time salary of £25,000. I knew this would increase our overall costs, which rose to £38,000. This required an extra £13,000 of support – more than £1,000 a month. My line manager had always been quite conservative, but we decided we could draw down some reserves, as I was only planning on doing a twelve-year term until 2022. Dipping into the reserves meant there would be no flexibility if a church reduced its giving. I felt a little under pressure to accept this new deal, but hoped and prayed it would all work out well.

My new deputy was running day-to-day operations from Germany, with another of our managers based in Switzerland and the other in Sussex. We started to meet quarterly for two days as a management team, instead of monthly for half a day. Each of us had a specific area of responsibility. Mine was speaker engagements, board management, vision, donors, and fundraising. Much of this could be done from home, and it gave me a role to focus on and a reason to live.

A difficult situation arose out of the blue when my home church advised me that my mission allowance was to be cut by

25% with immediate effect. I was taken aback, as I had shared my poor prognosis news with the assistant vicar only a few days earlier. As this was the first church visit I had received in thirteen years, I had imagined it would be entirely pastoral. I brought out the Jaffa cakes and tea, and nearly fell off the sofa at his second statement, which was, "and you will be retiring next April [2017]". "That's news to me!" I replied. So much for a pastoral visit… The vicar had started with, "Let's get down to business. You're not going to like this." He got that bit right, at least!

I was completely shocked, so I spoke to my church mission representative and a couple of friends who were on the mission board. They said they were so unhappy with the decision that they would stand down immediately. It seems the chair of the mission committee had perceived that I was not working enough during my chemo, advising the committee, "If she was in the NHS she would have been retired owing to ill health by now!" The error was that I *was* still working. CMS was very happy with me and my productivity, having stated that I could take as much sick leave as I needed. As it happens, I have always kept a log, and five years of doing double my paid hours had given me a generous bank of hours to supplement my actual hours if I had needed it. In reality, I have always juggled work and treatment. My care companion at chemo and I often did some work together while I had my infusion.

I appealed the decision, and my proposed early retirement was taken off the table. I'm not sure how it would have been enforced, as at the age of fifty-three I was fourteen years away from retirement! I negotiated a slight taper in the allowance cut, but was unable to stop the reduction altogether. I was told by the mission pastor that it was needed more by others. I decided to see whether I could raise the shortfall of £900 a month. It felt like no small sum when I also had in excess of £100,000 to raise a year for 28 Too Many. That said, I have been in mission since 2001, living by faith all that time. God has always met my needs, and I saw no reason why this season should be any different.

A few months after my proposed retirement date, another strange incident happened, whereby I was challenged by my church on the validity of my doctorate. The written challenges came frequently – sometimes weekly – for nearly nine months, with a number of spurious claims that were all completely unfounded. I was told I was not allowed to have anyone with me at any meetings about this, which was unhelpful (and probably unlawful, as a person with disabilities who has a government-approved personal assistant to help me navigate the complexities of work). I felt there were a lot of hoops to jump through, and that the devil had allowed jealousies and disunity to creep in. No wonder non-believers struggle when they see this behaviour going on in churches! Luckily, I found places and people who supported me, and took the situation to a level of authority where it could be dealt with. Sadly, I have never been used by my home church as a lay pioneer minister. However, I am blessed to have found other outlets for my skills, giftings, and calling. Was it all just spiritual warfare? That's a question for God when I get to heaven!

Art

One of the things I have always found helpful during challenging seasons is art therapy. I was lucky enough to have a year of this at North London Hospice shortly after my diagnosis, and found it was an excellent way to help me process my feelings. I was able to bypass my logical mind and let unprocessed feelings appear on paper, or in collage or clay – which then enabled me to see them clearly. I painted a few A3 pictures during the early stages of my chemotherapy journey while I waited for the official course to start. These pictures represented my PET scan, chemotherapy, the loss of management colleagues leaving 28 Too Many, and precious souls who have died that I am more affected by now that I have life-limiting cancer myself.

Through art therapy, I also illustrated how I initially felt about time running out and being given a limited amount of time, rather than assuming I would live to beyond eighty, or the full 120 years I had put on my financial advisor's plan (the maximum point on his spreadsheet!). I also drew out plans for my will, and used various art media to portray different aspects of my life and the challenge of living with more clearly defined mortality.

My twenty-five pieces of art became a turning point for me as I moved from losses in the present to the legacy I hoped to leave behind. It wasn't that I hadn't realized I would die before my diagnosis. I have a faith, and I believe this is a temporary time before eternity begins. Yet something messes with one's head when a consultant says, "I'm sorry, you have incurable cancer. Your prognosis is seven years."

Legacy

This new artwork collection mapped out a legacy of ten aspects of my life that I wanted to complete. I thought the first – my will – would be the easiest, but it was actually the hardest and took the most amount of time. This is partly because I have changed my mind from leaving money to lots of people to giving major gifts to fifteen charities, gifts of holidays to close friends, and treasured items to important people I love, including National Trust gifts to some (having purchased a membership in memory of my dad when I was twenty-one, which has continued to give me and many friends joy over the years). My will recently changed yet again, but then I finally had a concept that was worth taking to the solicitor.

The second legacy strand was my bucket list of twenty-five items. After my time in West Africa, this grew to a list of eighty-four places or experiences. I started putting them into action a month after my intense chemo treatment ended in January 2016, enjoying a one-hour ballroom dancing lesson in High Barnet with my flatmate and next-door neighbour. I also started a memory scrapbook, which friends sign when we complete a bucket-list activity together. This has guaranteed me at least one day of joy each month, however tough that month has been.

The third strand was the continuation of 28 Too Many. My twelve-year contract with CMS was set to end in 2022. This would take me to the age of sixty, my planned retirement age. It also takes me to the end of the seven-year prognosis, which means that, as was the case for my parents, I would not have a retirement. This is a tough one, as I don't really want to go without some sort of break from work, especially as I have been employed since the age of sixteen. As an added consideration, I cannot access my state pension until I am sixty-seven.

I hope to help create a succession plan for a new leader for 28 Too Many, allowing us to nest under another charity or finish our work as planned by the completion of the 10:10:10 vision. I am currently refining these plans with the chair and board, the management team, CMS, key churches, and valued friends.

The fourth strand was my lay pioneer minister (LPM) role. I met my vicar six weeks before diagnosis, and he affirmed my calling to healthcare chaplaincy. I used some of my thirty-two months of chemo to undertake the LPM application and training, complete any additional training required (CMS modules in chaplaincy and pastoral care) with Grief Matters to help grieving children and young people. I have the support of the diocese and my church in following this path.

I was licensed by Bishop Rob of Edmonton two years to the day from my graduation as a pioneer leader with CMS and the day after I received my cancer diagnosis. As so often happens, one door closes and another opens. This led to an honorary chaplaincy post at the Marie Curie hospice in Hampstead in September 2017.

I also met with my vicar to agree a new contract, whereby I would take Communion to four unwell women from the parish. Other aspects included funerals, preaching, and being part of the church leadership. The hospice and home-visiting roles have given me great delight.

The next strand was being accepted as a trainee oblate in the Benedictine Order. I had been visiting Malling Abbey – a community of Anglican Benedictine nuns – since 2008, while studying at ANCC. After seven years I was invited to become a friend of the abbey. In 2018, I was asked to undertake three years of training with Mother Abbess and some senior sisters, and was allocated to Sr Mary Michael as my new supervising nun. This involved attending two training retreats a year from 2018–20, which fitted in with the usual twelve annual retreat days CMS expected me to take. At the end of 2018, I moved from postulant to novice in the hope of graduating in late 2020, once I had kept my Rule for three years and been tutored with four others. We will continue to meet annually for life.

I am grateful that my cancer journey and resultant disability issues, particularly mobility and chronic fatigue, have enabled me to become an advocate in new fields. Having brought to fruition the "Please offer me a seat" badge, and seeing a quarter of a million produced in the first year of the scheme, I have become a transport advocate. I am also part of a CRUK and Imperial College Public and Patient Involvement Panel, assisting with clinical trial papers at Hammersmith Hospital. I have joined the panel of Independent Cancer Patients' Voice, and CRUK's involvement panel, helping with a 2021 Science Museum exhibition on cancer, a workbook for patients to help maximize health appointments, and training on speaking about usage of the intelligent i-knife, which is designed to detect cancers earlier. I have helped the National Trust by talking about legacy in its video on Claydon House, and spoken at the Institute of Fundraising's conference on creative legacy-giving. CRUK and the Mental Health Foundation would like me to do the same for them.

I started writing this book in 2019, which enabled me to use the year well, as I also unexpectedly needed a total hip replacement, identified after a bucket-list trip to Paris. I hope to write a memoir book after this and to make a memory stick containing highlights from my life.

The last four strands are all about the people I love. Firstly, I want to spend time with the friends and family members who mean the most to me. My inner circle has changed during my cancer journey, with a few people stepping back when their lives became more complex or simply went in a different direction. I have eight precious godchildren, along with a handful of others who are like godchildren, or are siblings of my godchildren. I want to spend time with them all, even though they are scattered across the world in Melbourne, Alabama, Sussex, Exeter, Manchester, and the Lake District. I also hope to pass on some of the lessons I have learned in my life so far.

One particularly underdeveloped strand is time for me! This is improving, as I am slowly becoming kinder about meeting my needs for sleep, mindfulness, peace, healthy food, space in my diary, and the absence of stress, anger, and toxic relationships. A small core of people support me in living well by delivering shopping, providing lifts to church, cooking homemade meals, accompanying me to appointments, making up medications, encouraging me to take a daily walk, managing my diary, and having me over for Sunday lunch. These friends are supporting me to stay at work, and are committed to helping me fulfil this legacy strand over the next three years. Since my hip replacement, I have doubled my household care assistance to four days a week.

The final strand is to create space for love, intimacy, and companionship. I'm not sure I am well enough for a full, committed relationship, yet I highly value three men with whom I have platonic relationships, and we occasionally holiday together. This space will be held open in case life becomes more balanced and I choose to prioritize this strand over those that will be completed by 2022.

I have become better at celebrating small goals in recent years. Each of my twenty-four chemo sessions was celebrated with the making of a glass bead to be placed on a long necklace. I will add more, if and when I need to, at a later date. I enjoyed making them, and it felt special – like someone ringing the chemo bell at the end of treatment.

I also feel losses much more acutely. I have faced so many physical losses, but it hurts much more than it really should when people overtly or covertly leave our friendship. Although intellectually I know that it is likely to do with what is going on in the life of the other person, my feelings are not as grown-up, and

I feel the pain deeply, both in tears and in my gut. I can no longer be who I was – that person has gone. I am a new normal; ever-changing and declining in health year on year. A brave smile and made-up face I may have – for myself as much as for others – yet I feel that people often want and expect the old me. Be angry with cancer, not me, I say!

Caring communities

My faith has greatly helped me cope with these challenges, and has not been dented. In fact, I wonder how I would have got through all these challenges without it. After recommitting to Christianity in late 1999, and heading off on my first three-month mission trip a week later, I stayed at HTB for about three years, then joined a church plant of St George's Holborn. I have stayed within the HTB pastoral group system to this day. I love the support it gives me, and the friends I have made and walked with over the last twenty years. I also went with all the HTB churches to the Home Focus summer camp, working in the children's and special needs children's team for five years.

In 2004, I felt God nudging me to move to a church closer to home so I could be more actively involved during the week. Having moved from South Kensington to Russell Square, becoming part of a church in Totteridge – which was only seven minutes by car or three tube stops away – was a great joy. This meant I could join, and later coach, the hospitality team, project-manage the building project team, attend Oasis healing and Thursday women's events, and go to morning and evening services for many years when I was not overseas. Church became a real rock in my life at this point.

Church has since become something I have inside me, rather than a place I need to be. I value a close community of people who can be like family to me. I am blessed to have found nine link churches committed to giving and praying with and for me, and for 28 Too Many, in Kent, Sussex, Hertfordshire, North London, Essex, and Cardiff. I aim to visit these churches every other year, along with attending CMS speaker events, conferences, and preaching visits.

I have found another church that acts as a place of refuge, where I can be available or not, rather than always being on duty. In addition to this, I have supervision for my anti-FGM and VAW work, and for my health issues, and to enable me to fulfil my hospice work in a healthy way, despite my personal diagnosis. I also have a counsellor who helps me process existentialist issues around facing my own mortality as well as the impact this has had, and continues to have, on relationships with colleagues, charity trustees, friends, tenants, caregivers, and church members.

Attending various courses and workshops has given me access to helpful information and lifted my spirits at times. A Cancer and the Workplace workshop helped me understand my rights and obligations, and how to communicate well with colleagues, bosses, and partner organizations. I also took part in a useful six-week Help Overcoming Problems Effectively (HOPE) course, where I met two women who subsequently joined the UCLH Macmillan Cancer Centre writing group.

Pioneered by Coventry University, and run across the country, HOPE is a good concept. The weekly sessions cover goals, thankfulness, skills, mindfulness, hand massage, reflexology, and journaling. I met some great people there who could relate to my world – in particular, the fact that I had spent six months at home to avoid infection.

I also attended an inspirational half-day workshop run by Look Good Feel Better. Founded by cancer survivors and supported by the beauty sector, the charity empowers women and men to regain their confidence while living with the disease. I sat in a room of twenty women – half bald, half with wigs on – and wondered what right I had to be there, as my hair had only thinned. That said, I still had tears streaming down my newly made-up cheeks, making rifts in the foundation and blusher. I felt as though I had been through a war of treatment, toxins, words, reactions, and isolation.

I used the course, and the bag of makeup, to build enough confidence to attend my first board meeting following four cycles of chemo. I put on high heels, a tailored dress, and a lot of make-up. It was the same technique I used for the *Good Housekeeping* awards photoshoot a week after a chemo cycle. I had never worn much makeup, but I now use it daily to make myself feel like me – the new me, that is; battered daily by appointments, reactions, procedures, and the stress of working through cancer. Every little tip helps the journey continue.

I enjoyed my two years at the writing group, which met weekly for up to two hours, with coffee and supper afterwards at the local cafe. It was a great support group, and I made half a dozen long-term friends. I wrote a couple of pieces each week and read them out at two tutor-run poetry recitals. I also organized a social event to see one of our actress members perform in *Witness for the Prosecution* – a play covering FGM.

I joined a photography group, hoping that once I had mastered some writing skills in the writing group and a couple of memoir workshops I would be able to illustrate this book with some of my photos or art therapy work. My PA, who had studied photography, joined me, along with a friend who is a professional photographer. Again, I made some excellent and very talented friends. I learned the basics, but long-term it was too technical for me, and I didn't have the time to practise with my increasing work portfolio.

I took 2019 as a sabbatical from all groups to focus on this book, and to decide whether I wanted to rejoin them or not. I did some advocacy work at the House of Commons in an attempt to pass a bill that would secure palliative care rights for carers and funding for those living with cancer. It was inspired by cancer patient Joy Watkins, who had given a rousing speech in the hearing of Enfield MP Bambos Charalambous. Unfortunately, the bill was never passed, and sadly I lost two friends from this group, including Joy herself. Like the others, they have not been forgotten.

The photography group was an extension of the art therapy offering at North London Hospice. I gained a lot from the hospice's offering of therapy, counselling, reflexology, massage, and acupuncture for pain management. The palliative care team has really taken care of me, right from being a group attendee on a sleep workshop through to home visits following my hip replacement. I feel pleased to know that I will be able to end my days there, or at the Marie Curie hospice where I am chaplain, and that I have attended both while in good health.

My final anchor place for care is Cherry Lodge, where I stayed immediately after my chemo in the summer of 2015. I have attended the evening lymphoma support group every six weeks ever since, which is run by a CNS. Only a ten-minute walk or bus ride from home, it feels like a safe place. I also attend acupuncture sessions provided by the founder, who was an A&E anaesthetist earlier in her career. I recently joined her and others on a Walk with Llamas outing – a delightful thing to do on a Sunday afternoon.

I enjoy doing extra helpful things for these charities: talking about my experiences to potential donors at fancy dinners and writing articles about how they are helping me lead a fulfilling life and create a positive legacy. I will leave all of these charities funds in my will.

Marathons

One of the most important items on my bucket list was a twenty-eight-mile marathon covering a route in the shape of Africa. We departed from my home at 9 a.m. on a stunning day in June, and it took twelve hours. Twenty-eight teams of up to six people either walked or ran a mile while pushing me in a wheelchair. The target was to raise £14,000, giving us £500 to complete and launch each of the twenty-eight country reports. We completed it in memory of the man I loved. He had said to his son as he prepared for surgery, "I'll either be with Jesus tomorrow or with Ann-Marie to help her complete her FGM dream." Jesus won – I can't really contest that!

The endurance of the 28 Too Many marathon teams was amazing, and I only stopped for one five-minute loo break in the twelve hours! One friend did the whole twenty-eight-mile walk, while another cycled with me. A friend and my PA drove a car full of goodies around, which acted as a support vehicle as they handed out info packs for each stage, as well as flags and T-shirts for every team member. Medals were awarded to each entrant at the closing ceremony. We smashed our £14,000 target, raising nearly £20,000 as a result of the amazing generosity of more than 100 friends, supporters, and kind families. Exhausted but elated, we celebrated our achievements under the stars and fairy lights in my garden until midnight, then headed to bed.

On another occasion I took part in a Santa Run. I left the starting line last, as I was in a wheelchair with a companion, but I walked the first, third and fifth kilometre and was pushed for the second and fourth. I couldn't believe how many people were on their second lap of Hackney's Victoria Park while I was still ambling around on my sticks. Every runner cheered me on with a high five, very much making me feel a part of the running community and super proud of my first medal. Never has a mince pie and bottle of water tasted so good as when I crossed that line. I swallowed both as quickly as I could and swiftly said a few words for radio about why I had taken part. Of the 350 participants, only one other was in a wheelchair. I would like to do the London Marathon one day, but would need to be pushed in my wheelchair, so that is a future goal!

I have only undertaken one other fundraiser, and that was for the physiotherapy I needed after my hip replacement. Although not a charity myself, I didn't want to end up in debt from raising funds to pay for my recovery. I am still paying off my student loan, as my income is minimal and my earning years are numbered. Again, nearly 100 people donated to this rather more controversial fundraiser. I have learned lessons from both events, as I continue to do in life – often getting things wrong, and quickly saying sorry if I have a chance to do so!

NINE:
LOOKING TO THE FUTURE

In 2019, I started to think about options for the future of the charity, and also for myself. By then I had worked in corporate life for fourteen years, then eleven years as a consultant, followed by fifteen years in aid and charity work. Factoring in the years up to 2022, this would make forty-three years of working life, starting from the age of sixteen. Over nearly five decades, I have worked and trained professionally in HR, marketing, counselling, coaching, psychology, aid work, church ministry, and chaplaincy. This has been a huge privilege, and has given me an understanding of many disciplines, including banking, retail, finance, private-sector business, government, housing, and various public-sector charities.

The challenge when it comes to short- and long-term planning is that my health is unpredictable. The prognosis I was given in 2016 only takes me up to 2022. Being a pragmatic optimist, I am assuming I will have the full seven years and hoping I will be in the tail of the standard bell curve and live much longer. My parents died during their early sixties without enjoying any sort of retirement, so I hope to finish my legacy (seven years) and then enjoy less active and goal-focused time – or to at least more leisure and pleasure.

One of the challenges when I was first diagnosed was that I couldn't see myself living beyond the immediate work years of 2022, or sometimes even past the thirty-two months of chemo. I have always been a visionary and a planner, and had hoped to take on various social projects during my retirement, including training to become a magistrate, prison visiting, and serving as a volunteer tour guide at the Victoria and Albert Museum; and, for pleasure, travelling to the other half of the world that I have not yet visited, and studying for an art history or art therapy degree. I had to rethink my options and evaluate which dreams were still possible, and then see what could be factored into my seven years of working life. The silver lining is that, for all the doors that have closed, others have opened.

I chose to keep working through my chemo to ensure that the charity kept going, to give me something worthwhile that was bigger than me to focus on, and to save any sick leave in case I really needed it further down the line. Having appointed Sean as my deputy, 28 Too Many was back on a fairly stable path from spring–summer 2016, and I was pleased that I managed to keep attending the board and strategy meetings – even though one of each was by Skype, owing to a broken hip in the summer of 2019.

I look back on some of my significant graduation and licensing moments with great gratitude. The day of my licensing as a lay pioneer minister at St Barnabas Church in July 2017 brought a great cause for celebration, with all my greatest friends invited. Many made very sacrificial journeys from Dorset, Sussex, the Lake District, Kent, Nottinghamshire, Coventry, Birmingham, Brighton, Manchester, Switzerland, Hertfordshire, Buckinghamshire, and more! I felt it was important to say my vows publicly. I also felt that, by hearing them, those people had vowed with me, so that when the going got tough I could go back to them for assistance, support, and prayer.

Bishop Henry Scriven, visiting bishop to CMS, washed my feet. This was symbolic, humbling, and memorable. He had asked me before the service if I was wearing tights. I answered, "Why, do you need them for a fan belt?!" He replied, "No, just to wash your feet, as Jesus did for his disciples!" I blushed and blamed the cancer diagnosis I had received the day before.

Bishop Rob, who had licensed me, introduced me to the lead chaplain at the Marie Curie hospice in Hampstead. I had an interview with him and the head of facilities, and was given a tour of the hospice. They made the bold and brave decision to take me on, despite my cancer diagnosis. We chose not to share this diagnosis with the staff, as I didn't want to be treated differently from other professionals in the patient and family support team (social workers, bereavement team, counsellors, psychologists, chaplains, and administrators) or the wider team of facilities and support functions, nursing and medical staff, or, ultimately, the patients.

In the first few months I noticed that every week a patient I had seen the week before was no longer alive. Every Tuesday evening I lit a candle and wrote about what I had learned from that patient and how his or her life had blessed mine, and then let the candle burn down overnight. Writing about how I felt enabled me to process the number of people who were dying in my life, as well as my own mortality.

It was as this point that I started seeing a spiritual director every six weeks to further process the work and talk over any faith issues. In addition to this, I had team supervision (spiritual reflective practice) – initially weekly with my manager and then monthly as the team grew. I was the first honorary (volunteer) chaplain to join, and was later joined by a female Anglican priest, a trained chaplain from a Salvation Army background, a man from a Catholic context with community experience, and a Buddhist monk with hospice experience.

One of the highlights of my Tuesday work day was an hour-long exploration of one or two patient cases, where we could explore our feelings, consider their treatment options, and understand something about their family and background. These reminded me of the grand rounds, or "Schwarz Rounds", I used to take part in at Charing Cross Hospital medical school, where staff spoke on various interesting topics. I took part in one of those panels at the hospice and found it to be a great training experience for speaker and audience alike, though of course there was also a lot of sadness involved.

One of the annual traditions at St Barnabas is for all ordained and lay ministers to go for replacement of anointing oil on Maundy Thursday at St Paul's Cathedral, and then for lunch afterwards. I do this annually now and find it a delightful service, with ordained and lay clergy from across London.

My LPM licensing opened up new doors, extending the journey I had taken with the pioneering team at CMS. It meant I could join the National Anglican Community of Pioneers, represent Anglicans at interfaith meetings, and lead funerals in robes. It also gave me the chance to write a chapter in Cathy Ross's *Pioneering Spirituality* and to be quoted in Elaine Storkey's *Scars Across Humanity*.

My weekly attendance at the Marie Curie hospice is for work only; I have kept my own treatment at North London Hospice to maintain professional boundaries. It was for the latter that I undertook the Santa Run in 2017, raising £750.

Another new experience I found really interesting was visiting the death cafés created by Dying Matters. Facilitated by a trained person and volunteer, between fifteen and thirty people came to the two I attended at North London Hospice's Health and Wellness Centre. The range of attendees was broad, including a funeral director to an eighty-year-old friend of a cancer sufferer, a blogger to a community befriender, a researcher to a cancer survivor, and a widow to a carer. Any question could be asked, and all the dialogue took place over excellent homemade cake and copious amounts of tea – just my sort of gathering! Survivors have to be fairly robust, but this was a good way of opening up dialogue on dying, which will happen to us all. I would definitely attend again, and felt it was good for a couple of survivors to be at each event to help educate and answer questions, although there is obviously no such thing as a standard survivor.

Having entered my fifties, many friends of a similar age have lost their parents, either to cancer or to other causes, including motor neurone disease, unsuccessful organ transplants, late-stage Parkinson's Disease, and pneumonia. I have supported three close friends, on separate occasions, in the Chapel of Rest to provide comfort and prayer.

I didn't see my father after he died, although I wanted to, and I later regretted it. I was with my mother as she took her last breath. I have been there almost at the end with other friends, and with many cancer patients. I have benefitted from, and greatly put to use, my cross-cultural studies training from ANCC, and my experience and learning of other faiths – particularly Judaism, Catholicism, Islam, and Buddhism – at these moments.

Among the challenges I have faced over the last four years with cancer include the slow decline in my mobility, stamina, mental cognition, and memory. I have decided that it is all about adapting, just like living in different overseas contexts, so I use no sticks in the house, one all the time outside, two sticks for proper walks, and a wheelchair for museums, parks, holidays, and so on.

I have also had to accept a daily regime of medication, including steroids, painkillers, bone protection, opiates, nerve blocks, stomach protectors, regulators, and migraine (post-forced menopause) medications. These are split over ten doses taken between 7 a.m. and 10 p.m. I aim to sleep eight to ten hours a day (one eight-hour sleep and a two-hour nap) and to work flexibly when my cognition and stamina are at their best, sometimes lying in bed for comfort. I am trying to get my sleep pattern back to 11 p.m. to 8 a.m. as a regular base, yet I am a natural night owl on steroids!

Since the summer of 2019, I have had to accept more care and have added another two hours of light housework to the existing cleaner and gardener support. I have an amazing PA who supports me in my work and ensures that I take my meds, eat and rest well, and don't burn out. We also have two interns this year in advocacy, and a care/palliative/FGM intern who gives me one evening of care a week. These are supplemented by caregivers, who, between them, make up seven weeks of medication; deliver shopping; cook, box up, and deliver three meals and desserts each week; accompany me to key results appointments and infusions requiring anaesthetic; and accompany me home when I cannot drive.

I have also had to cope with an increase in diagnoses linked to the cancer, chemo, or both. These include osteoporosis; forced menopause; pelvis, femur, and hip degradation; jaw necrosis; and sight, hearing, taste, and appetite loss due to nerve damage post-chemotherapy. This means I have to manage a healthy diet while trying to enjoy some quality of life and monitoring daily blood sugar levels.

I have two more medical procedures planned: a second total hip replacement, likely in the summer of 2021, and a stem-cell transplant at three weeks' notice if (or when) the disease progresses again. As the latter will be the third of my four lifelines, I need it to be as far off as possible. Believers hope and pray for a miraculous cure, as I do, yet I also need to be pragmatic given my diagnosis of life-limiting and incurable late-stage cancer.

The future of 28 Too Many

As I have said, my original plan when I created the charity was to produce research reports for the twenty-eight African countries affected, and to see a 10% reduction in prevalence in ten countries over a period of ten years. That initial plan will have been completed and far exceeded by the end of the ten years. In addition to the twenty-eight country reports, we have produced twenty-eight model law reports to be used by the few countries that currently have no anti-FGM legislation, have not passed the drafted law, or still need to implement it. This will cover countries that follow English, French, and Sharia law principles. We have already produced specialist thematic reports on medicalization, law, and social norms. We expect to publish further thematic reports on the link between FGM and diasporic populations, the role of faith, and key statistics and general trends.

We approach the new decade with a new chair and plans to recruit a new treasurer. With a stable board and three populated subcommittees (focusing on governance/selection; fundraising with key donors, regular committed givers, and individuals; and finance), this is a good time to start discussing the future of 28 Too Many. I intend to relinquish my role as executive director in late 2022, twelve years after joining CMS, ten years after founding the charity, and seventeen years after meeting Fatima in West Darfur.

The board will need to cover the executive director's salary after this, as my role has been self-funded through CMS, and will also need a team administrator, as my PA has been financed by a government grant since 2015. I feel the new executive director will need to be good at strategy and leadership, fundraising, and speaking at churches and conferences. This person will need to have a passion for the cause and be prepared to work antisocial hours, since speaker engagements are usually at weekends and in evenings. I believe the post needs to be held by a woman, and possibly one from a BAME background; ideally from an FGM-practising community. Owing to my illness, Sean has been running the day-to-day operations. Both roles could possibly be fulfilled by one full-time person now that the systems, finances, payroll, and website are set up.

The options for the charity are to stay as it is, recruiting a number of key postholders, or to merge with an existing anti-FGM charity. We will explore both options in 2021. We could also join a larger NGO, such as Plan International, Save the Children, or Amnesty International, as a specialist department. The issue with this option is that charities like these tend to follow the funding, and FGM is not always blessed with consistent long-term grants.

It costs between £150,000 and £200,000 a year to run the charity. The first £100,000 a year we raise covers the personnel, research, office, web communications, UK and international advocacy, and travel costs. The second £100,000 covers research development, translation, teaching and training, and resource development. We would love to grow this second income stream so we can extend our work.

We have plenty of ideas for scaling up our work – not only to the twenty-eight countries in Africa, but also to the countries that practise FGM in South East Asia, such as Indonesia, and areas populated by the Bohra people group in India and Pakistan. FGM is also practised in parts of the UAE, Iraqi Kurdistan, and Colombia. We would like to undertake country reports in these countries, and in all diaspora countries where people have settled with populations that practise FGM.

We are looking to replicate our country reports and training resources, and to ensure that they are available in every appropriate language for ease of access. We would like to encourage corporate donors to use some of their corporate social responsibility budget to help fund this replication and translation project. We would also like to partner with relevant organizations to make sure that these relationships benefit the organization and its employees.

Another option would be to create a research institute, broadening our research into other geographical areas. While this is an appealing option, it comes with the need to lecture, publish, and supervise PhD students. I am currently the only one with a doctorate, although our three other managers have master's degrees. This option would also require serious funding, but it would be the best guarantee of a legacy, as it would enable us to keep all our current reports updated and produce more. In an ideal scenario, we would partner with around five other global universities to create this research institute. The next round of DFID anti-FGM grant funding is soon to be allocated. We would need £3 million of the £50 million on offer, but we don't expect to receive it. We will see whether we are successful as a technical advisor to one of the consortia. Alternatively, we would need a few philanthropic or corporate donors with a significant corporate social responsibility (CSR) budget to allocate to us.

The final option is to close. My team and I know this is a possibility, and from a personal perspective it is fairly appealing, as I would leave with my vision fulfilled. That said, I could see my baby being nurtured by other parents if it continues, growing to a teenage and then to an adult stage of development. I also have the option to stay on as ambassador/founder, which would give the charity access to my fundraising assistance. There are many decisions to be made, and in the end it will probably come down to the personnel involved.

Before leaving the charity for good, or morphing into an ambassador, I would like to ensure that it has a good financial standing and can continue its work, fulfilling my God-given calling to end FGM for all time.

What next?

My roles as honorary hospice chaplain and disability advocate are expected to extend beyond 2022. I can stay under the CMS umbrella at least up to my normal retirement age of sixty-seven. I may go from my current one day a week at the hospice to two, or keep my work pattern as it is, with one day for lay pioneer minister work under the Bishop of Edmonton.

It may be hard for some to believe this, but my work at the Marie Curie hospice is one of the most enjoyable aspects of my life. In addition to the induction and mandatory annual training, I have trained in dementia care and as a hospice biographer, enabling me to record narrated stories from those approaching the end of their lives. The memory stick offered to relatives afterwards is a precious way of ensuring that memories continue into the next generation of friends, family, and godchildren. Barbara, founder of The Hospice Biographers, has offered to write my biography, which I will record at home in 2021.

I produced a radio report for The Hospice Biographers' radio station with my art therapist from North London Hospice. I also appeared on a live radio show, and would quite like to do more of this work – an opportunity that was offered after my first appearance. In addition to this, I took a chaplaincy module at CMS, a pastoral skills course, and a grief course with Grief Encounter. We will see where these opportunities lead.

I have trained as an honorary chaplain or faith volunteer at the Royal Free Hospital in Barnet. My chaplain has trained me to run funerals, especially where the family has limited funds and a local authority cremation is offered. I have assisted with three so far, and will soon be conducting these on my own.

I very much enjoy taking Communion to the sick and dying, either at home or in hospital, and I have ministered to four women from my home church over the last three years. I have seen two women recover and two die. I also visit patients from my cancer support groups (lymphoma, photography, and writing) when they are unwell.

I recently attended a celebration service at my church, along with two partner or plant churches. A new pioneer curate has joined us for two years and will lead a church plant to Colindale. I have joined in with his vision and am part of a core group of interested persons. I feel excited about this possibility, even if I am only well enough to be an intercessor.

I can also see the church's local estates-based ministry to Strawberry Vale and the Grange expanding to train estate-based leaders who have no formal theological and leadership training. I completed my one-year ANCC placement at Strawberry Vale and have been looking out for a role I could play. I think I could mentor a young person monthly for eighteen months and also offer some skills training with the church-planting curate. This would give me a role in my church, which has, up until now, been slow to materialize. Perhaps God wanted me to wait and rest, knowing it would come to pass. I also needed to write this book and recover from my hip surgery. This has enabled me to evaluate where I am and figure out what I would like to do next.

From my legacy plan of ten strands set in 2015, this book, my legal will, and a plan for 28 Too Many will be completed. The other work areas of disability advocacy, lay pioneer ministry, and Malling Abbey will continue for life. My bucket list will be completed and replaced with a wish list, and the three personal areas of time devoted to loved ones and leisure will continue to be prioritized.

TEN:
MY NEW NORMAL

As a friend helped me proofread some of the early chapters of this book during the first weekend of January 2020, news was just emerging of a little-known virus in Wuhan, China. We mailed off the printed manuscript the following week and waited for the next step in the process.

January 2020 started with great expectation for the decade ahead. We had two interns join us at 28 Too Many: one studying neuroscience (two years) and another studying politics (one year). We spent much of the beginning of the year preparing for our attendance at the United Nations Commission on the Status of Women (CSW64) in New York in March, where we planned to meet policy members, government representatives, and other NGOs to campaign for changes in law and support for those affected by FGM.

My PA and I had attended the Civil Society Forum (a pre-event in Geneva, in October 2019), at which CSW marked the twenty-fifth anniversary of the Beijing Declaration (the 1995 road map for the empowerment of women and girls). This helped me keep FGM on the agenda of international statutes and clarify some of the focus for the forthcoming event. We planned to take a team of six to New York from 9th to 20th March 2020 to join the twelve other speakers we were hosting. The last time I had been there was in 2012, when we were just setting up the charity.

We had successfully pitched to hold three prestigious side events. First, we were to host an international panel of speakers on social norms, showcasing a report we had put together in late 2019 at which our trustee, Mama Sylla – FGM survivor and chairwoman of La Fraternité Guinéenne – was to speak with our Kenyan FGM ambassador, Esther. Second, we planned to host a panel to launch 28 Too Many's FGM Model Law report on International Women's Day. Third, we were to host a panel with a politics intern speaking to me and others on the role of men and boys in the fight for equality and in ending FGM.

We made a good start to our work with a strong International Day of Zero Tolerance for FGM on 6th February. We marked the one-year anniversary of the #NoFGM campaign, which we had launched in 2019, and attended an event at the House of Lords to encourage MPs to show solidarity with Sierra Leone, alongside the Rescue Children and Youth Film Foundation, and the Hawa Trust. Information about this event, led by male activists, was shared across the Sierra Leonean press.

Pandemic

By the end of February, we had launched new short reports on Cameroon, Ghana, Chad, and the Central African Republic, and had also had a successful Anti-FGM Day. We had spent much of the month finalizing our flights, accommodation, visas, bookings, speeches, event plans, and UN passes, as well as liaising with our speakers, who would be flying to CSW64 from various part of the USA and Kenya.

Italy had declared an international public health crisis in January because of Covid-19. Its claims that the virus would be over by April seemed unlikely, as the World Health Organization had declared it a pandemic. Italy swiftly went into "lockdown", a term we would hear often in 2020. To make things more challenging, I had broken my foot in January following an eyesight crisis and was expecting to travel to New York wearing an orthopaedic boot on one foot.

On Thursday 5th March, we heard that the US government was refusing to let us and thousands of other UN delegates travel to New York because of the pandemic. With just two days' notice, our flights for the Saturday were cancelled. We dusted ourselves off and made plans for a virtual Model Law report launch instead. We had no idea that the UK would also be in lockdown by 23rd March.

In those two intervening weeks, I had no outside contact except for a few medical appointments and a haircut. We just managed to film my contribution for a Press Red film on FGM – a series of resources about gender-based violence and abuse against women and girls, entitled *Turn the Silence Off*. Little did I realize that I had somehow caught Covid, so for the first eight weeks of lockdown I was ill with the virus that was spreading globally, like our own living version of the movie *Contagion*. From late March to late May, I had two weeks of breathlessness and fatigue, two weeks of acute kidney pain and gastric issues, two weeks of a chickenpox-like rash and a further two weeks of acute fatigue. As if that wasn't enough, I split my lip after slipping in the shower, as I had started to experience poor eyesight. This prompted home adaptations to keep me safe and I ended up having to "shield" at home for nearly a year. I had little choice in my small world, without even a PA on hand, as she was also shielding.

Covid had taken less than 100 days to shut down the world, with many lives lost and many conspiracy theories abounding. On the plus side, we heard birdsong, noticed shyer wildlife, and enjoyed cleaner air once again. Activities to look forward to included tea or drinks over the fence at the weekend, clapping for the NHS on Thursday evenings, and watching Joe Wicks's fitness videos, even though they were aimed at children. I grew vegetables, enjoyed eating lunch on a tray in the garden, and discovered Netflix, Shakespeare, and opera online.

With the heir to the throne and the prime minister both diagnosed with Covid, I was glad we had not flown to New York and been marooned there, but I felt extremely sad that we had been unable to attend CSW64, and that all our preparations had been wasted. We held our virtual launch of the FGM Model Law report and, amazingly, the Sudanese government passed new legislation outlawing the practice, despite us not going to New York. This was the highlight of 2020 for me, giving girls in a country with one of the highest rates of FGM a level of protection. It has been fifteen years since I met Fatima in Sudan, and this outcome means a great deal. I sincerely hope it will protect her grandchildren from FGM. I smile even now at this extraordinary answer to prayer.

In April I embraced a new home office, while my PA also needed to work from home with her husband and three-year-old. Given my sight loss and mobility challenges, it was difficult not having an on-site PA. I registered for Age UK and Royal Volunteer Service volunteer support, and have also had a great group of volunteers from my church, link churches, and friends helping me. By the early summer, I was allocated three new volunteer cooks via a Covid-19 volunteer hub, who delivered a box of pre-cooked food daily. This carried on until early August, then moved into another form of support, as people were no longer passing by en route to church, music lessons, work, and the like. One family is still supporting me, as is a wonderful charity called One Stone House, as I am not well enough to cook a meal each evening.

After the New York trip was cancelled, our communications team began to offer online advocacy and social media workshops to our network of activists in East and West Africa, as local programme support had been cut because of Covid. We also became a key player in providing accurate information for the UK Metropolitan Police, US Border Force, and other police services via a bi-monthly Covid intelligence-gathering call regarding global FGM and related violence against women, especially across Africa, the diaspora, and in the UK.

I had to let my newest tenant go, as I could not have anyone in the house while I was shielding. This immediately halved my income – on top of the fact that my previous two tenants had left the year before owing to Brexit and other global uncertainties. Places of worship closed and I spent a quiet Easter watching Holy Week unfold online. I kept an eye on my inbox as events and conferences were cancelled. It felt very surreal and eerily quiet as we worked out how to refocus, embracing Zoom communications for all our meetings.

The impact of Covid was scary at times. By the end of the summer we had lost the brother-in-law of one of our colleagues to the disease, as well as the fathers of three of my friends. I was unable to volunteer at the Marie Curie hospice, which had established two eighteen-bed wards – a Covid one and a non-Covid one – to support the NHS health crisis in London. Meanwhile, the Nightingale Hospital was built at the ExCeL London convention centre as a standby that everyone hoped we wouldn't need. In parallel, Covid testing was becoming available and scientists were working hard to develop a vaccine.

My invitation to join a Buckingham Palace garden party celebration marking the 125th anniversary of the National Trust very sadly disappeared, as did my monthly bucket list of treats, holidays, and retreats. Yet, as I thought of disappointments like this, I was aware of those having a much worse time. Footballer Marcus Rashford shone the spotlight on child food poverty, as, without access to free meals during the school holidays, underprivileged children were going hungry. With personal experience of child food poverty, Marcus spearheaded a campaign to extend the government's free school meals over the Easter and summer holidays during the 2020 lockdowns. His relentless pressure on the government paid off, as children in need were eventually provided with free meals during the holidays. Marcus is inspirational and has become my superhero!

The media brought to our attention the horrific death of George Floyd, and the need to give the Black Lives Matter movement a huge amount of extra awareness.

In the months that followed, we were encouraged to "eat out to help out" the hospitality sector. Huge segments of our lives inevitably ended up online, and because of this it was only possible for those with IT bandwidth to stay connected, identifying the poverty divide in our society once again.

By the end of June, we realized that 28 Too Many had lost 25% of its funds, as I was not travelling to churches to speak, and some donors had stopped giving for economic reasons. We were in a worrying financial position. As I had learned from my cancer diagnosis five years earlier, uncertainty breeds further uncertainty. Two of our long-term team members left in the summer, and we still miss their input and contribution to our work. This, plus our financial situation and my health issues, meant we had to reconsider our future. Our board's Summer Away Day and Management Strategy Day were dedicated to appraising our options.

As summer arrived, school exams were cancelled and we switched to a completely online presence. We worked closely with the UN and used our media contacts to promote the plight of women and girls at risk behind closed doors as Covid spread across Africa. We shared our intelligence on FGM and child marriage with the relevant agencies. Our ambassadors and activist partners shared how financial hardship and FGM were increasing as a precursor to child marriage. This was seen as a way of reducing economic hardship related to girls' education costs and the provision of food. All forms of abuse have soared behind closed doors – due, directly and indirectly, to the pandemic. Many charities and local NGOs have also become insolvent due to funds being redirected to Covid efforts. It may take decades for the progress I have seen, in terms of FGM rates dropping over the last twenty years, to get back on track.

By the end of July, my diary was busier than it had ever been, with ten events taking place a week, in addition to webinars, conferences, meetings, and training. I was online for around twelve hours a day, from Sunday to Friday each week, never leaving my house.

August heralded my release from shielding. In reality, I was still cautious, maybe due to the fact that I had been at home for five months by then. A backlog of health appointments meant I needed sixteen hospital visits or tests – three medical visits a week for a month. I was offered several retreats, courtesy of friends from Buckinghamshire, Hertfordshire, Dorset, and Sussex, enabling me to enjoy outdoor picnics in St Albans, Hatfield House Park, Trent Park, and the Leckford Estate. My PA and I managed to meet in the garden of our local carvery and at the Courthouse Park's outdoor café. In fact, the latter became my venue of choice over the summer for a weekly coffee and cake with my carer or with a local friend at the end of a walk. My only other trip out in August was to attend the funeral of a very dear friend in Warwickshire. We had been peers on our cancer journey, and I am still grieving her passing. We held a memorial service for her via the writing group at the end of the summer.

I signed up to an RNIB sight loss service, which enabled me to receive the week's news in audiobook form and to join Barnet's sight-impaired group. My grey walking sticks were replaced with white ones and my doctor approved an application for a guide dog. It is hard to keep moving owing to my deteriorating health, but without access to the usual distractions, recuperation, and rest I used to get from holidays, retreats, and regular company, getting around makes me feel as empowered as possible.

I have maintained my Benedictine Oblate office prayers each morning, midday, and evening. I also listen to Classic FM all day, which offers restful stress reduction. I thoroughly enjoyed all three episodes of Gareth Malone's *Great British Home Chorus*, which clearly demonstrated the benefit of singing for key workers and those who were shielding. I could relate very well to this. This prompted me to learn to record myself – even if it was only by taping my phone next to the words on my computer while a recorded backing track played on a different device!

I also loved the two projects I undertook with Chicken Shed Theatre. For the first, I was anonymously paired with a young paediatric nurse in Manchester for four weeks of letter writing before we met virtually on Zoom. This project, Living Letters, was designed to facilitate intergenerational dialogue between two people who were shielding. My second project, The Space Between Us, enabled young people and seniors to share memories of a life well lived, as well as hopes, fears, joys, and experiences. It was pure joy!

Fully back at work in September, we focused on our annual review, which was to be shared at our October AGM and on closing the last financial year's accounts. We also recruited two new communications team members to cover general communications and graphics work, and a Kenyan ambassador to manage social media. We later recruited a new research project manager to carry on with our research programme, which was due to be completed by April 2021. We also began working on a significant research project for an external NGO, focusing on what works across their programmes, and ultimately elsewhere.

Our AGM went well, and we welcomed three new trustees to replace two who were moving on after three or four years on the board. We were also very pleased to launch our mobile app, enabling greater access to our research on the part of activists and NGOs in Africa, particularly in rural locations. A number of us have been heavily involved in our #Challenge28 fundraising campaign, aiming to raise £28,000 to enable the charity to keep going after April 2021. We will see! By January 2021, we had raised £7,800 and received a pledge of £14,000 to match up to 50% of what we raise!

By October, local mayors across the UK were challenging the tier system. All too soon, the area of London I live in moved from Tier 2 to Tier 3, and then all of London moved to Tier 4. None of this made much difference to my life, although I had enjoyed a few visits to church prior to this, when up to sixty people were allowed to attend for a few weeks. I enjoyed a very special relationship with a family I had "bubbled" with, meaning that we were able to enjoy walks, ice cream, and coffee in the park, as well as celebrating three birthdays (including my own lockdown birthday), episodes of *Strictly Come Dancing*, Christmas, and New Year, with a bit of English teaching and a few sleepovers thrown in. I have loved joining them and reading stories, making crafts, sharing experiences, praying, and having tea or dinner together once a week. I get my fix as an extrovert and share of love in exchange!

By November and December, the news was filled with talk of vaccines and rules to keep, break, or flex. I attended nine more funerals and one Zoom wedding. I also chose to declutter my loft with the help of two volunteers from North London Hospice, who visited for five two-hour sessions. Then I had to wait until the charity shops reopened to donate all my unneeded items. By the end of the year I was very tired, so I took a couple of weeks off after the Christmas office closure to recuperate.

Another of my aims in 2020 had been to address the perpetrators of abuse in my life and to ensure that other victims would be protected. This took a lot of investigation with the police, HR departments, NHS facilities, schools, and the Catholic and Anglican churches. Needless to say, I will rest more easily at the end of my life knowing this is sorted. I managed to finalize my end-of-life paperwork, feeling a sense of relief as I filed my will. I would recommend this to everyone, as one never knows when the end is nigh. Having enjoyed helping to plant a church in North London in 2019, I hope to join some new church activities once things open up again.

Following all this activity, I took some courses in mindfulness – Twelve Steps in Celtic Spirituality, the Alexander Technique, and Emotional Spirituality – to feel refreshed and achieve a better work-life balance.

I was blessed to be given my first dose of the vaccine in early 2021, which allowed me to volunteer as a hospice chaplain again.

Lessons learned

One of the lessons I have been learning through all this is the value of transparency and integrity, and the importance of showing understanding and compassion to colleagues. As this decade unfolds, we will all need to adapt to the new status quo in education and set appropriate ethical boundaries. This will have an effect on our world, country, environment, and social organization. I hope we will be able to apply the lessons learned from this pandemic at 28 Too Many as we continue our life-changing work.

CONCLUSION

I have identified five key themes while writing this book. These are important to me, as they have formed me into the person I am today.

Hardship and not fitting in

The first two relate to hardship and not fitting in. I was born to wartime parents and working-class grandparents, who moved from Manchester and Birmingham to a leafy cul-de-sac in an affluent area of rural Buckinghamshire. As a bright only child, I was too clever to fit in with my peers, and my parents prioritized the education they had not had themselves by sending me to a convent school.

As a non-Catholic who was less well-off than the other children– with a working mum and a hired car for school runs – I felt different. Being abused by a priest further isolated me, and experiencing inequality for women while working at the bank, and then racism while on holiday in Zimbabwe, helped forged my career choice of equal opportunities within HR. My path to fight against injustice for the disadvantaged, marginalized, and disabled was set.

Grief and loss

The next two themes in my life relate to a large amount of

grief and loss. My only grandma and my class teacher died the year I was abused at school, aged around seven or eight. My parents died of cancer when I was in my twenties, along with my next-door neighbour, who had acted as a grandma. Most of my uncles and aunts died while I was at school, and when my husband left, just after my mum's death, his family all followed suit except for one cousin. Synagogue life ended, as did my job, career, and health. But within a few years I had regrouped, retrained in neurolinguistic programming, found Christianity, and set up my own business. My calling then was to work with the most disadvantaged in society and to pass on knowledge.

I was known as "Pollyanna" at school, and I was an obvious fit for Brownies and the Red Cross by the age of six. Helping via medicine appeared to be my career path until a friend's sister took her own life when we were fifteen or so, after which the friend and I both left school at sixteen. I made a choice to join the bank where her father worked as a director, having made the decision that I could help people through HR, not just medicine.

After my parents' deaths, I retrained in counselling, coaching, and psychology. A breakdown at thirty made me want to help others avoid losing their careers and lives, and I took this vision to the developing world as a volunteer for five years. Once I had come face to face with FGM, I discerned that as my new life calling.

The convent nuns had been very significant to me in terms of their faith influence, but also in their values of diligence, compassion, obedience, poverty, and love for those on the margins. We were encouraged to donate a share of our weekly pocket money to the mission boxes, which, along with my mother's bookkeeping lessons at the age of six, helped me become a good steward of my assets. Perhaps it is not surprising, given their influence, that I wanted to train as a healthcare chaplain and lay nun (Benedictine oblate) during my retirement. These roles were simply brought forward by my health challenges. The bank also instilled in me the lesson that I would lose my job if I went even a penny overdrawn – one many would benefit from today!

Legacy

The last theme relates to legacy. As a female only child, I knew I would end the Wilson line in name once I married. I took my husband's name, yet when I was awarded Freedom of the City of London, it annoyed me that I was described as "the divorced wife of [my husband's name]". I went straight from Guildhall to my solicitor and changed it back to my maiden name. I will now keep my family name for the remainder of my days! As my parents died young, without any need for institutional care, I inherited their assets. I lost half of my inheritance in my divorce settlement, which was heartbreaking. However, my parents' savings guaranteed me a home while I had little income.

My will has proved challenging over the last five years. The newest draft will mostly benefit charities, as most of my friends and extended family have earned enough during their own lifetimes. I also plan to set up a foundation to help those needing small loans for educational purposes, which they can pay forward once they have earned enough to repay the capital.

My own sense of legacy enables me to prioritize the ten areas I set shortly after my diagnosis. I will step back from 28 Too Many in the next few years, feeling that I have played a key role in ending FGM. My aim is that I will have completed this book and be trained as a Benedictine oblate and chaplain by 2022. What remains after that will be bucket-list items; time with family, friends, and godchildren; and time for myself and the causes I champion. These continue to give me a sense of joy and closure.

Top tips

Often when I speak at churches, people ask me; "How do I find my calling?" For me, calling is the strand that runs through the centre of something. Picture a stick of seaside rock. Calling is the bit that says "Brighton Beach".

In 1999, shortly after I came into a deep knowledge of what it meant to be a Christian believer, I felt my calling was to work with the most disadvantaged in society and pass on knowledge. By 2005, my vision was to help end FGM by creating a knowledge portal of tools and creating change via top-down and bottom-up strategies. These two visions or callings have a similar base, yet the latter is narrower in focus. I would not have arrived at the second without the first, however. I hope this book inspires many to find and fulfil their God-given calling. This could include parenting, study, all types of paid work, volunteering, helping others, self-employment, self-sufficiency, religious orders, community living, and many other options.

My strong sense of calling has made it easier to prioritize my time and resources in order to fulfil certain goals or projects, while also giving me the ability to decline others. This has become more and more important in light of my recent health challenges. Ironically, I have never been a great worrier because I see little point in being anxious about something that might not happen, and because, based on experience, the issues I have worried about have not come to pass, while others have occurred instead. My top tip for anyone wanting to follow their calling is to look at their major achievements. Review lessons learned and impacts made, successes actioned and challenges overcome, and reflections forged along the path. Then be bold enough to try new things – just do it!

It is very important to have a circle of wise advisors and prayerful intercessors around you if you are considering mission so you can ask difficult questions and remain accountable. It is also good to consider what would happen if you followed your calling… and if you didn't! It's important not to run away from anything, even though the mission field can be a tough, isolated, lonely place – where poor mental health strikes the strongest as well as the most fragile souls. A good sending agency and a church backer are essential. It is also a good test to see if you can fundraise for your project. If you can't, the chances are the project is not needed! God sometimes shuts doors like these, as frustrating as it can be.

Finally, know that nothing is wasted. I needed all my education and experience to set up and lead 28 Too Many, often leaning on skills I had learned in the Red Cross or Territorial Army, or from my psychology studies. Without the confidence gained from these roles, I would not have had the courage to contribute to the North and South Sudan peace accord in even a small way. I still made mistakes, especially during my early days in Kosovo, but they were all learning experiences for the next step.

The challenges of my calling

Meeting Fatima was my Esther moment; the day my life changed forever. I view the rest of my life as either before or after that. I am pleased that I did something about FGM, giving up all my security, status, and income to pursue a very different life. I am also very pleased that I joined CMS. This organization has always understood me and my pioneering spirit. I had to pioneer FGM into its thinking, and then again into my church's thinking, yet CMS has worked with and supported me for more than ten years. It has also been useful to have more than thirty years' work experience behind me, which I can access as and when it is needed.

I believe that God's voice set me on this path. After birthing the call, it had to be tested and confirmed by others. Then I had to skill up, which involved a tough internship in northern Pakistan, learning basic midwifery. I feel extremely fulfilled knowing that I delivered six babies there and four in northern Nigeria. Along with my eight godchildren, I feel as though I have had fulfilment enough on the child front for one lifetime!

The refining of my initial call and a conceptualization of the 10:10:10 strategy followed. I envisioned a simultaneous top-down and bottom-up squeezing of the problem, supported by a one-stop-shop portal where all the vital information on FGM could be found.

It feels as if this call to help end FGM followed directly from the wider calling to work with the most disadvantaged in society and pass on knowledge. Therefore, college placements at our local Strawberry Vale housing estate, teaching English at a Christian community women's project in Luton, and working in Dadaab, Kenya, fitted within the wider call, and added to my skills and experience as the strategy for 28 Too Many was being incubated for birth. For me, as the vision-caster, it has been a privilege and a challenge to maintain the initial call with successive staff, volunteers, and board members. It has also been important to ensure that mission creep did not happen, to avoid stretching our tight personnel resources and exactly-enough-yet-no-more financial resources beyond our core plans. It is only in the last few years that we have considered undertaking research in the Middle East and Asia.

The challenges I experienced early on included some clear closed doors, which were useful for discerning the right path to take. For example, I broke my foot in Kenya, having just returned from West Darfur, and as the civil war had worsened by the time it healed I was unable to return to Sudan. Other doors opened, and although I was offered a year's rest at ANCC, I completed a three-year degree in two years, preparing me well for my long-time path in mission. When my church required me to find a sending agency, it appeared to be a real challenge – but, after taking various courses to show that I was psychologically well, I received five offers, and my church helped me select the best fit.

I still believe I was right to go to West Africa before receiving my cancer diagnosis, as I have not been able to return to Africa since. I still carry memories of the toughest aspects of Kenya: the attack and rape of my colleagues at gunpoint, whom I helped debrief, and the thousands of FGM stories I heard, alongside witnessing other things no one should ever have to see. Though I have overcome these challenges, they have left their scars.

Other challenges to overcome included losing my parents during my twenties and my marriage ending before I was thirty.

Yet not having any dependents meant that I could advance my psychology and cross-cultural studies, and then just go! I often wonder what my parents would have thought if they had lived to see their daughter achieving these things after leaving school at sixteen.

I remember aid workers advising me not to make emotional attachments to local staff, beneficiaries, or projects, yet I kept a soft heart, despite the tough work. If I hadn't, I could not have befriended a vulnerable homeless man called Josef while I was volunteering for a Healing on the Streets project with St Barnabas in 2009. When I asked this well-dressed man how we could pray for him, he shared that he was homeless. A male team member and I took him out for lunch and he poured out his story. In time, I found him a flat and helped him enroll on two college courses. Sadly, his health took a bad turn and he died suddenly. I was there when his body was found, and I later returned to administer last rites with a vicar, as well as breaking the news to his family. I planned his funeral, took a work team to clear out his flat, and collected his ashes to be buried in the UK and in Portugal.

I would not have been able to fulfil my honorary chaplaincy role without keeping a soft, compassionate, and easily hurt heart. Yet this is not always seen by others, many of whom see only the tough exterior. As with trees, there are many layers to my personality, and only those who are trusted get to see the inner rings. Despite these successes, my soft heart still grieves the loss of key staff or colleagues who moved on from the charity for personal reasons.

The other challenge or obstacle I have found tough is the sector's politics. All of us at 28 Too Many aim to get on with everyone, to never criticize others or other organizations, and to be true to our agreed values of respect, compassion, excellence, honesty, and pioneering.

As for roadblocks that might have stopped someone less determined, getting cancer and facing many other issues connected to it has to come in at number one! Having thirty-two months of chemotherapy, yet still juggling a full-time role, health appointments, writing a book, and training in lay pioneer ministry, chaplaincy, and as a Benedictine oblate, has taken some planning and dedication over the last five years. My strong sense of legacy made it easier to focus on how I use my time and assets – even for holidays, completing my bucket list, and spending time with friends, family, and godchildren.

CMS has been very helpful in helping me navigate through the challenges of an unexpectedly reduced annual donation from my sending church. I also leaned on CMS's assistance and coaching from a donor's coach to help resolve some perceived contractual issues with an ex-board member.

Key successes

There have been some amazing successes of working in partnership with other anti-FGM charities and the survivor movement. We are unique as the only faith voice, so although our charity is faith-neutral, I can speak at certain events as a woman of faith. This has also brought challenges, such as the time we were offered a partnership with a donor who was marketing sex aids and wanted to put our logo on his products.

We are very pleased to have been the UN's IAC representative for the UK, and to have been chosen by the UK government to collect 300 signatures from faith leaders for the first FGM summit (the Girl Summit in 2014). We were honoured to partner with Ogilvy & Mather on a free FGM campaign that went viral, aired on French TV, and won Global Advertiser of the Year at the Clio Awards.

The other awards I have received have also been a huge encouragement. Although given to me personally, they really recognize the work of our whole team. I was humbled to receive a British Citizenship Award and an Inspire award from the Evangelical Alliance, as well as being chosen as a heroine by *Good Housekeeping*. Memories of my makeover day and treat weekend for the latter will remain with me forever, and cream teas at the Houses of Parliament and Lords for the other two will also remain lifelong treasures.

I am pleased to have helped get FGM into the Sustainable Development Goals (SDGs) in the early days, and into the NHS GPs' coding book of conditions, so there is now an official medical code for FGM and related complications.

A couple of very generous donors have been essential in sustaining our financial viability and our success, and I will be eternally grateful to them. We were also delighted that anti-FGM collective Vavengers chose to support our schools' pack.

I have enjoyed meeting some amazing people along the way. My meeting with Pope Francis in Rome is at the top, along with meeting the first lady of Burkina Faso, the archbishops of Canterbury and York, Dr Hamlin at the Addis fistula hospital, and Jenni Murray on *Woman's Hour*. Going back to my old school forty years after leaving to lead an assembly on FGM was another highlight. I am also really proud of our blue #NoFGM ribbons to help the sector unite under one globally identified logo and message.

Some of my greatest field successes included following British teacher Lydia's work in Uganda and addressing a multi-thousand-strong audience about FGM. Working with Cricket Without Boundaries and the Maasai Cricket Warriors in rural Kenya, and with our Mali country coordinator Gemma to host the first FGM network meeting in Mali, were also highlights. I feel blessed to have travelled to 60% of the world, and to have seen minimal change in my life since being diagnosed with cancer. Yet my life has of course changed, as have the lives of those closest to me.

Under normal circumstances, I would not have trained as a chaplain while fulfilling a full-time role, but I used untaken leave during chemo to complete the training needed. I am so pleased that Bishop Rob suggested I volunteer at the Marie Curie hospice in Hampstead, as I have met many wonderful patients and staff through this role. I am also proud that the "Please give me a seat" badge I conceptualized was accepted by Transport for London. More than 250,000 have been produced so far, and every time I see one in use I smile.

I imagine I will continue to pioneer new projects. I am

currently volunteering with CRUK, Independent Cancer Patients' Voice, Transport for All, and the Public and Patient Involvement Panel at Hammersmith Hospital with Imperial College. I have stepped back from the UCLH Macmillan Cancer Centre writing group and the North London Hospice photography group, but hope to resume these at a later stage. My post-2022 wish list continues, and I hope to maintain a varied life for as long as I can.

How you can get involved

Having read up to this point in the book, you can now be involved in helping to end FGM once and for all. We have worked with various regional branches of the Women's Institute, Mothers' Union, Zonta International, and Soroptimists. If you are a member of one of these, or Rotary, or a girls' brigade, school, or university society, please consider adopting us as one of your causes.

We would love to equip a UK squad of trainers to deliver talks in schools, health units, universities, churches, faith buildings, corporate settings, and so on. We would also be delighted to train a UK-wide group of advocates to ask questions of their MPs, support GP practices with information, and attend events run by UN women, UNICEF, or other key bodies and institutions. We would like to set up dinner clubs where FGM can be discussed based on a podcast or MP3 message we would produce containing relevant material and questions. A group would then have a monthly dinner, learn about and discuss the issues, take some advocacy action, and share knowledge with others. The funds saved from going out for dinner – £15 or $20 per head – could then be sent to the charity. Alternatively, this book could be bought and read as a book club choice to educate and inspire.

Our charity needs to share its reports across the world until all six billion people on the planet know about FGM and want it to end. We want people to share reports within their networks in the diaspora, and with contacts in Africa and elsewhere, and we would like to recruit a network of country ambassadors and friends to help support our work.

We have very few donors who give monthly. We would love you to donate the cost of your lunch one day a week or your takeaway coffees via standing order. Without regular, predictable funds, we will not be able to expand and complete all our work as planned. The funding situation will be even more precarious once I have left.

We have had great success from a wide range of individuals fundraising for our charity. These have ranged from learning to play an instrument to celebrating a fiftieth birthday, running a marathon, half-marathon, or 10K – including me and many others taking part in the 28 Too Many wheelchair marathon, which raised nearly £20,000. This latter project raised enough to cover the production of all remaining fourteen country reports. We would encourage individuals to be creative in raising funds as leisure groups, students (RAG committees or societies), professional or church women's groups, youth or justice groups, and so on. We will provide support, a T-shirt, and a JustGiving page, so please commit to one of the ideas above or your own initiative.

If everyone who bought this book set up a small monthly standing order to 28 Too Many, we could most likely guarantee our future sustainability. That way my efforts in writing this book will not have been wasted, and my legacy will continue after I am gone. Even if I don't live long enough to see FGM completely ended, you just might! Together we can save one girl from this unnecessary and harmful practice every five seconds, and end FGM for good.

FURTHER RESOURCES

- www.28toomany.org/research-resources
- www.28toomany.org/donate
- www.nofgmribbon.info
- www.churchmissionsociety.org/people-in-mission/
  ann-marie-wilson
- www.un.org/sustainabledevelopment/gender-equality
- www.macmillan.org.uk
- www.mariecurie.org.uk
- www.mallingabbey.org